TOWARD MORE GLORIOUS PRAISE

Power Principles for Faith-Filled People

Jack W. Hayford

with

Dr. Tom McDonald

THOMAS NELSON PUBLISHERS
Nashville

CONTENTS

Toward More Glorious Praise: Power Principles for Faith-Filled People is one of a series of study guides that focus exciting, discovery-geared coverage of Bible book and power themes—all prompting toward dynamic, Holy Spirit-filled living.

About the Executive Editor

JACK W. HAYFORD, noted pastor, teacher, writer, and composer, is the Executive Editor of the complete series, working with the publisher in the conceiving and developing of each of the books.

Dr. Hayford is Senior Pastor of The Church On The Way, the First Foursquare Church of Van Nuys, California. He and his wife, Anna, have four married children, all of whom are active in either pastoral ministry or vital church life. As General Editor of the *Spirit-Filled Life Bible*, Pastor Hayford led a four-year project, which has resulted in the availability of one of today's most practical and popular study Bibles. He is the author of more than twenty books, including *A Passion for Fullness*, *The Beauty of Spiritual Language*, *Rebuilding the Real You*, and *Prayer Is Invading the Impossible*. His musical compositions number over four hundred songs, including the widely sung "Majesty."

About the Writer

TOM McDONALD has served as Minister of Music at Trinity Assembly of God in Baltimore, Maryland, for the past nineteen years. Through his growing ministry there, in conference work, and frequent lectures at colleges and seminaries, he is becoming widely respected in his field of Church Music.

Tom is a graduate of Essex Community College (A.A.), Towson State University (B.S./M.Ed. in Music Education), and did his doctoral studies at The Union Institute (Ph.D., 1993). His work has been rewarded with awards, including the Governor's Award of Excellence (1988), and he received the Outstanding Young Man in America Award twice (1982, 1989).

He and his wife Denise have two sons: T. Michael (10) and Christian (4). Of this contributor, the Executive Editor has remarked: "Tom McDonald is a refreshing departure among skilled and well-trained church musicians. He retains a pursuit of excellence always, but mixes it with a human warmth and accessibility that keeps music relevant to the most common worshiper, as well as to the most musically sophisticated."

THE KEYS
THAT KEEP ON FREEING

Is there anything that holds more mystery or more genuine practicality than a key? The mystery: "What does it fit? What can it turn on? What might it open? What new discovery could be made? The practicality: Something *will* most certainly open to the possessor! Something *will* absolutely be found to unlock and allow a possibility otherwise obstructed!

- Keys describe the instruments we use to access or ignite.
- Keys describe the concepts that unleash mind-boggling possibilities.
- Keys describe the different structures of musical notes which allow variation and range.

Jesus spoke of keys: "And I will give you the keys of the kingdom of heaven, and whatever you bind on earth will be bound in heaven, and whatever you loose on earth will be loosed in heaven" (Matt. 16:19).

While there is no conclusive list of exactly what keys Jesus was referring to, it is clear that He did confer upon His church—upon *all* who believe—the access to a realm of spiritual partnership with Him in the dominion of His kingdom. Faithful students of the Word of God, moving in the practical grace and biblical wisdom of Holy Spirit-filled living and ministry, have noted some of the primary themes which undergird this order of "spiritual partnership" Christ offers. The "keys" are *concepts*—biblical themes that are traceable through the Scriptures and verifiably dynamic when applied with soundly based faith under the lordship of Jesus Christ. The "partnership" is the *essential* feature of this release of divine grace;

(1) believers reaching to *receive* Christ's promise of "kingdom keys," (2) while choosing to *believe* in the Holy Spirit's readiness to actuate their unleashing, unlimited power today.

Companioned with the Bible book studies in the *Spirit-Filled Life Study Guide* series, the Kingdom Dynamic studies present a dozen different themes. This study series is an outgrowth of the Kingdom Dynamics themes included throughout the *Spirit-Filled Life Bible*, which provide a treasury of insight developed by some of today's most respected Christian leaders. From that beginning, studious writers have evolved the elaborated studies you'll pursue here.

The central goal of the subjects focused on in this present series of study guides is to relate "power points" of the Holy Spirit-filled life. Assisting you in your discoveries are a number of helpful features. Each study guide has twelve to fourteen lessons, each arranged so you can plumb the depths or skim the surface, depending upon your needs and interests. The study guides contain major lesson features, each marked by a symbol and heading for easy identification.

 WORD WEALTH

The WORD WEALTH feature provides important definitions of key terms.

 BEHIND THE SCENES

BEHIND THE SCENES supplies information about cultural beliefs and practices, doctrinal disputes, business trades, and the like, that illuminate Bible passages and teachings.

AT A GLANCE

The AT A GLANCE feature uses maps and charts to identify places and simplify themes or positions.

 KINGDOM EXTRA

Because this study guide focuses on a theme of the Bible, you will find a KINGDOM EXTRA feature that guides you into Bible dictionaries, Bible encyclopedias, and other resources that will enable you to glean more from the Bible's wealth on the topic if you want something extra.

 PROBING THE DEPTHS

Another feature, PROBING THE DEPTHS, will explain controversial issues raised by particular lessons and cite Bible passages and other sources to which you can turn to help you come to your own conclusions.

 FAITH ALIVE

Finally, each lesson contains a FAITH ALIVE feature. Here the focus is, So what? Given what the Bible says, what does it mean for my life? How can it impact my day-to-day needs, hurts, relationships, concerns, and whatever else is important to me? FAITH ALIVE will help you see and apply the practical relevance of God's literary gift.

As you'll see, these guides supply space for you to answer the study and life-application questions and exercises. You may, however, want to record all your answers, or just the overflow from your study or application, in a separate notebook or journal. This would be especially helpful if you think you'll dig into the KINGDOM EXTRA features. Because the exercises in this feature are optional and can be expanded as far as you want to take them, we have not allowed writing space for them in this study guide. So you may want to have a notebook or journal handy for recording your discoveries while working through to this feature's riches.

The Bible study method used in this series revolves around four basic steps: observation, interpretation, correlation, and application. Observation answers the question, What does the text say? Interpretation deals with, What does the text mean? —not with what it means to you or me, but what it meant to its original readers. Correlation asks, What light do other Scripture passages shed on this text? And application, the goal of Bible study, poses the question, How should my life change in response to the Holy Spirit's teaching of this text?

If you have used a Bible much before, you know that it comes in a variety of translations and paraphrases. Although you can use any of them with profit as you work through the *Spirit-Filled Life Kingdom Dynamics Study Guide* series, when Bible passages or words are cited, you will find they are from the New King James Version of the Bible. Using this translation with this series will make your study easier, but it's certainly not necessary.

The only resources you need to complete and apply these study guides are a heart and mind open to the Holy Spirit, a prayerful attitude, and a pencil and a Bible. Of course, you may draw upon other sources, such as commentaries, dictionaries, encyclopedias, atlases, and concordances, and you'll even find some optional exercises that will guide you into these sources. But these are extras, not necessities. These study guides are comprehensive enough to give you all you need to gain a good, basic understanding of the Bible book being covered and how you can apply its themes and counsel to your life.

A word of warning, though. By itself, Bible study will not transform your life. It will not give you power, peace, joy, comfort, hope, and a number of other gifts God longs for you to unwrap and enjoy. Through Bible study, you will grow in your understanding of the Lord, His kingdom and your place in it, and those things are essential. But you need more. You need to rely on the Holy Spirit to guide your study and your application of the Bible's truths. He, Jesus promised, was sent to teach us "all things" (John 14:26; cf. 1 Cor. 2:13). So as you use this series to guide you through Scripture, bathe your study time in prayer, asking the Spirit of God to illuminate the text, enlighten your mind, humble your will, and comfort your heart. He will never let you down.

My prayer and goal for you is that as you unlock and begin to explore God's Book for living His way, the Holy Spirit will fill every fiber of your being with the joy and power God longs to give all His children. So read on. Be diligent. Stay open and submissive to Him. You will not be disappointed. He promises you!

Lesson 1/The Call to Worship

All across the land, a new breeze is blowing. There is, in the Christian church, a fresh interest in worship. This interest is observable in both the pulpit and pew. Everyone is talking. Renewal is in the air.

Those who postulate church trends indicate that across the board, regardless of denominational stripe, believers are hungry for an authentic experience when they gather to worship. Welton Gaddy writes, "Worship is fundamental. Worship is the foundation of everything else the church is doing."[1] This hunger to worship God in biblical correctness and purity is a natural response to the condition of our time.

Our society is confused. Looking for answers, people gallop from fad to fad, hoping aimlessly for satisfaction. It is no wonder that amid such trendiness, the people of God are beginning to march to a different drummer. And the Bible is clear:

• "Where sin abounded, grace abounded much more." (Rom. 5:20b)

• "'Not by might, nor by power, but by My Spirit,' says the LORD of hosts." (Zech. 4:6b)

• "As the deer pants for the water brooks, so pants my soul for You, O God." (Ps. 42:1)

• "Some *trust* in chariots, and some in horses; but we will remember the name of the LORD our God." (Ps. 20:7)

As our culture becomes increasingly chaotic, the Christian must adapt a worldview clearly centered in the "I AM" of Scripture (Ex. 3). We are to be "in the world but not of the world" (see John 17:14). Therefore, as Richard J. Foster has written, "If the Lord is to be *Lord*, worship must have priority in our lives."[2]

The essence of this contemporary call to worship is found in the ability to prioritize worship as the central activity of life and then to make it significant by embracing biblical patterns. For a life empowered by vibrant worship is a clear witness that Christ's resurrection is truth, not fiction.

In that regard, let's investigate the biblical precedents for God's call, which include viable implications for both worship and service.

UNDERSTAND THAT GOD CALLS

Throughout Scripture, God has called persons "for *such* a time as this" (Esth. 4:14). If we believe that a fresh call to worship the Lord is in the land, we must initially understand that God calls "to" Himself, before releasing an individual "to do" in His name. Formation precedes vocation.

Read the following scriptures. What has God called all of us "to"?

Deut. 13:4

Josh. 22:5

 AT A GLANCE

Truth Joshua Teaches	Action Joshua Invites
Steps to Dynamic Devotion Joshua continues to call God's people to devote themselves completely to the Lord. In a day when so many follow the Lord with only partial devotion, Joshua and Caleb, "who wholly followed the LORD" provide challenging examples of the life the Lord honors.	**Be careful** faithfully to apply all of God's Word to all of your life. **Follow** Him with all of your heart and soul.[3]

Ezek. 44:15

Mark 12:30

1 Thess. 4:7

What has God called us "from"?

Ps. 34:13

Prov. 3:7

Gal. 5:19–21

Col. 3:5

 AT A GLANCE

Truth Colossians Teaches	**Action** Colossians Invites
Keys to Godly Relationships Human relationships were designed to be fueled and filled by righteousness. To the degree we give in to the urging of our flesh nature, we will fail to experience righteous or fulfilling relationships. To the degree we practice those things God commands, our relationships will become a sampling of heaven on Earth.	**Reject, turn from,** and **refuse to practice** any form of relational unrighteousness or sin: wrong sexual activity, angry exchanges, jealous or envious attitudes, greedy desire for things, gossip, or coarse humor.[4]

What are some biblical promises for those who follow the call of God?

Rom. 6:23

Rom. 8:1

Rom. 8:37

1 Cor. 10:13

 ### WORD WEALTH

More than conquerors, *hupernikao.* From *huper,* "over and above," and *nikao,* "to conquer." The word describes one who is super victorious, who wins more than an ordinary victory but who is overpowering in achieving abundant victory. This is not the language of conceit, but of confidence. Christ's love conquered death, and because of His love, we are *hupernikao.*[5]

2 Cor. 12:9

 ### FAITH ALIVE

In the world, talent reigns supreme. An actor who is compelling on screen may feel no particular responsibility to behave uprightly in private. In the kingdom of God, however, a different accountability system is in vogue. Character is valued. The private life affects the public ministry. Therefore, a premium is placed on obedience to the Word of God evidenced in a purposed resistance toward evil. We are called to die to the flesh, so that the Spirit may live. Decidedly, we decrease so He can increase. The Christian is called to a

value-driven system of conduct. This, of necessity, must pre-
cede the call to worship or service.

REALIZE THAT GOD'S CALL IS SIGNIFICANT

We must be aware that when we hear the call of God, and
choose to obey that call, we set in motion certain behaviors.
Any call of God presupposes a holy life-style, in terms of character and conduct. Before we can worship "in spirit and truth"
(John 4:24), we must relinquish sin and serve the Savior. Consider the following questions:

How did Jesus explain the exclusivity of our worship of
God? (Matt. 4:10)

How did Paul describe "all who in every place call on the
name of Jesus Christ our Lord"? (1 Cor. 1:2)

What did Paul say should govern Christian relationships?
(Col. 3:15)

How did Peter bring closure to the significance of our
call? (1 Pet. 2:9)

WORD WEALTH

Chosen, *ekletos.* Compare "eclectic." From *ek,* "out of,"
and *lego,* "to pick, gather." The word designates one picked
out from among the larger group for special service or privi-
leges. It describes Christ as the chosen Messiah of God
(Luke 23:35), angels as messengers from heaven (1 Tim.
5:21), and believers as recipients of God's favor (Matt. 24:22;
Rom. 8:33; Col. 3:12). The New Testament traces the source
of election to God's grace.[6]

FAITH ALIVE

Priority of Worship. As a "royal" priesthood, the kingly nature of the redeemed worshiper is noted. [First Peter 2:9] is rooted in God's call to ancient Israel (see Ex. 19:5–7). Peter and John (Rev. 1:5, 6) draw this truth to full application and prophetic fulfillment in the New Testament believer. As with Israel, deliverance through the blood of the Lamb is but the beginning. As promised, dominion and destiny will unfold as their priestly duty is fulfilled. True authority is always related to a walk in purity and a constancy in worship. The spirit of worship is essential to all advance of the kingdom. Just as ancient Israel will only take the Promised Land while doing battle from a foundation of righteous worship before the Lord, so with the contemporary church. We will only experience promised power for evangelism and spiritual victories as we prioritize and grow in our worship of the living God. Kingdom power is kept from pollution this way, as kingdom people keep humbly praiseful before the King—and witness His works of power with joy.[7]

LEARN FROM THE PAST

Two giants of the faith—Moses in the Old Testament and Paul in the New Testament—are fitting examples of men who heard the call of God. From two passages of Scripture, let's lift spiritual principles related to the call of God.

Read Exodus 3:1–12 and learn from the call of Moses.

Verses 1–4:

Was Moses alone when God spoke to him from the burning bush?

Was that experience expected? Was it routine?

In similar fashion, as we walk with God in contemporary times, we may hear from Him in a manner totally unexpected. We cannot forecast a burning bush, but we can anticipate a burning bushlike encounter. Be aware. Be available. Be sensitive.

The routine of "tending the flock" may be transformed into an environment of great power and insight, should God Almighty choose to break through onto our scene.

Verses 5, 6
Why was Moses instructed to remove his shoes?

What is the significance for us in terms of our approach to God in worship?

It is important that we examine our attitude when worshiping God. He is holy. He is to be revered. His name is the name above all names. His deeds are righteous. He will not look upon sin.

Let's take a reality check. When did you last "take off your shoes" (figuratively speaking) while in His divine presence? It is inappropriate to enter into His presence with a cavalier attitude and simply expect His attention and favor.

Verses 7–12
How did God acknowledge His concern about His people?

   WORD WEALTH

Know, *yada.* To know, to perceive, to distinguish, to recognize, to acknowledge, to be acquainted with; in a few instances to "know intimately," that is, sexually; also to acknowledge, recognize, esteem, and endorse. When Scripture speaks of God's making known His name, it refers to His revealing (through deeds or events) what His name truly means. Thus, in Exodus 6:3, "I appeared to Abraham, to Isaac, and to Jacob as *'El Shaddai,* but *by* My name *Yahweh* I was not known to them," God did not mean that the Patriarchs had never heard the name *Yahweh,* but rather that He did not reveal the full meaning of His name *Yahweh* until the time of Moses and the Exodus.[8]

What was His plan?

Through whom is He to work?

What was Moses' response?

Upon hearing Moses' response, what did God say?

It is paramount to remember that when God calls us to a role of service, He enables us for the task. His call is awesome, but so are His abilities to empower.

 FAITH ALIVE

Have you had a "burning bush" experience in your pursuit of God?

Are you willing to encounter one in the future?

How would you like to respond should *you* encounter a similar experience as Moses did? Explain.

Now read Acts 9:1–9 and learn from Paul's unusual and dramatic conversion and call. This powerful account highlights his immediate response. Compare the physical impact of Paul's encounter with God to that of Moses' encounter.

When Paul heard the words of Jesus, how did he respond? (v. 6)

What was the commission given each man—Paul/Moses?

Whom did God send to each man to help him following the miraculous encounter?

Often we only know in part what the will of God is for us when we first hear His call. The issue is our willingness to follow blindly—to abandon our routine and accept His will. From the lives of Moses and Paul, we can learn an important spiritual principle relating to the call of God. Simply stated, these two fathers of our faith chose to listen and voluntarily obey. No hidden agenda. No debate. No preconditions. God called, and they responded.

IN SUM

Throughout the Scriptures, God's call came to ordinary persons like you and me. Having heard the call, their lives were transformed through their obedience to the voice of the Lord.

Today, we perceive that God is calling once again. As we hear the voice of God, may we respond as did Isaiah when the Lord called him to be a prophet:

I heard the voice of the Lord, saying:

"Whom shall I send,
And who will go for Us?"

Then I said, "Here am I! Send me."
—Isaiah 6:8

1. C. Welton Gaddy, *The Gift of Worship* (Nashville, TN: Broadman Press, 1992), 58. Used by permission.
2. Richard J. Foster, *Celebration of Discipline: The Path to Spiritual Growth* (New York, NY: HarperCollins Publishers, 1978), 140.
3. *Spirit-Filled Life Bible* (Nashville, TN: Thomas Nelson Publishers, 1991), 341, "Truth-in-Action through Joshua."
4. Ibid., 1821, "Truth-in-Action through Colossians."
5. Ibid., 1701, "Word Wealth: 8:37 more than conquerors."
6. Ibid., 1910, "Word Wealth: 2:9 chosen."
7. Ibid., "Kingdom Dynamics: Priority of Worship."
8. Ibid., 87, "Word Wealth: 3:7 know."

Lesson 2/Are You Willing?

Moses is an interesting example of a man who risked everything in order to pursue God's call. Think back to when Moses first noticed a bush that crackled with fire without being consumed—then paused and moved closer (Ex. 3). He was certainly curious; yet there was something deeper and more profound at work. He willingly stepped *closer* first, to risk the power of the presence of God. It was voluntary. God called and he responded, "Here I am."

The act of a human willingness to move toward the Lord always signals blessing. It is the first step in meaningful, divine dialogue. Metaphorically, a door opens; and amazingly enough, notwithstanding our human weakness, we control both the speed and trajectory of the opening of the door. Our attitude moves or stymies the hand of God.

When God first calls, we have multiple options, namely:

1. We can stiffen our necks, connoting that everything is fine in our lives—"Thanks, God, but I really do not need You now," so to speak.

2. We can choose to ignore the voice of God and selfishly pursue our own wills, our own activities.

3. We can even attempt to placate the call of God, saying in effect, "Let me see what You want, and if it is win/win for me, I'll pray about it!"

All of these choices are clearly prideful, self-serving, and utterly foolish. They represent a spiritual sort of Russian roulette—a game in which we have elected to take a chance on our finite knowledge, when we could take full advantage of God's infinite wisdom.

On the other hand, however, we can choose to willfully obey God. Individuals who respond positively to the call of God exhibit three valuable behavioral traits:

1. They demonstrate *sensitivity* to God.

2. They are clearly *serious* about God's enterprise throughout the world.

3. They are *teachable*—open to receive instruction and counsel.

The following examples from Scripture will amplify this definition.

TWO MARYS: SENSITIVE WHEN CALLED

Mary the Mother of Jesus

The ageless account of Mary the Mother of Jesus is a story that baffles both innocent children and cynical adults in terms of its beauty and devotion. Mary heard the call of God, and immediately she became sensitive to the intent of Gabriel's message. She opted for obedience.

Read Luke 1:26–28. What did the angel say to young Mary? (v. 28)

Although Mary was an ordinary woman, in secular terms, why do you think God chose her for such an extraordinary responsibility?

What are the implications for you and me in terms of hearing a call from God, even though we may perceive our own "limited resources"? (v. 37)

After hearing the angel, Mary "was troubled at the saying" (v. 29). What was the significance of the angel's response? (v. 30)

Personalize that verse to your own life.

Finally, what did Mary say? (v. 38)

How important is her response? Explain.

 AT A GLANCE

Truth the Synoptics Teach	Action the Synoptics Invite
STEPS TO FAITHFUL OBEDIENCE Obeying the Father was supremely important to Jesus. Obedience is the response of faith to any instruction from God. Jesus taught that true faith will always be manifested in obedience to God's revealed will. Successful Christian living results from seeking and knowing God's will and then doing it in faith.	**Adopt** Mary's attitude. **Submit** your plans to God's will.[1]

 KINGDOM EXTRA

Faithful Mother: Obedient Disciple (Mary). There is a wonder surrounding Mary, the mother of Jesus [Luke 1:26–56], that transcends traditional religious thought. That she was a privileged vessel, chosen to bear God's Son, is wonder enough, for she is a participant in the miracle of the Incarnation at a level no other human being can comprehend. It is clear that she did not claim to understand it herself, but simply worshiped God in humble acknowledgment of the phenomenon engulfing her existence: "My soul magnifies the Lord," she exclaims (v. 46). We can hardly fathom the bewildering moments she experienced 1) when Simeon prophesied future mental/emotional suffering (2:35); 2) when she and Joseph spoke with Jesus after they thought He was lost in Jerusalem (2:49, 50); 3) when Jesus gently rebuffed her at the wedding in Cana (John 2:4); 4) when Jesus seemed to reject her and His brothers' efforts at helping Him, though they clearly misunderstood Him at that time (Matt. 12:46–50). These instances prompt our learning the wisdom of persistence and obedience in following God's basic directive on our lives, even when the details on the outworking of His will are unclear to mystifying.

Mary is also a study in the pathway forward in God's will. She might have sought elevation in position among those who saw Jesus for who He was—Messiah—but instead 1) she remained steadfast with Him all the way to the Cross, rather than protect herself (John 19:25); and 2) she obediently joined other of Jesus' disciples in the Upper Room, waiting as He commanded for the coming of the Holy Spirit (Acts 1:14).

Mary is a model of responsive obedience, one who lived out her own directive to the servants at Cana—timeless advice for all ages: "Whatever He [Jesus] says to you, do it" (John 2:5).[2]

MARY, THE SISTER OF LAZARUS

This Mary was a devoted disciple of our Lord. Her willingness to tangibly demonstrate her love personifies the sensitivity of which we are speaking. She was able to transcend the normal duties of the day and to intuitively be led by the Spirit. Her action bore tremendous symbolism and insight. She heard a different kind of call . . . a call of the Spirit enabling her to honor our Lord amidst sharp criticism and confusion.

Read John 12:1–8. What was the perfume Mary used? (v. 3) How is it described?

What in your life, or among your possessions, would you be willing to sacrifice to bless our Lord or to further His church's mission?

What was Jesus' response to Judas's criticism? (vv. 4–8)

It is interesting that this story is told in all four Gospels (Matt. 26:6–13; Mark 14:3–9; Luke 10:38–42; John 12:1–8), underscoring its relevance for our lives. Compare all four accounts and create your own outline of this "worship" encounter.

From the lives of these two women—Mary the mother of Jesus and Mary the sister of Lazarus—we may learn the value of being sensitive to the call of God; to be sensitive in the presence of God as well.

Mary's love in pouring perfume was risky. But as Max Lucado has commented, "the rewards of risky love are always greater than its cost. Go to the effort. Invest the time. Write the letter. Make the apology. Take the trip. Purchase the gift. Do it. The seized opportunity renders joy. The neglected brings regret."[3]

Take some time here to introspect on the two Marys: How can you become more like Mary the mother of Jesus in your response to the call of God?

the call of God to worship?

Are you ready to risk more, as Mary, Lazarus's sister did, in order to demonstrate your love of Christ?

How will this attitude affect your worship from now on?

ABRAHAM AND DAVID: SERIOUS WHEN CALLED

Abraham

Abraham, the Old Testament patriarch, was serious about the call of God. He could not be trapped in possessions, locale, or friendships. When God spoke, Abraham obeyed. Consequently, the blessing of the Lord on Abraham's descendants is a matter of historical record. A critical element of Abraham's life-style was worship—time alone in listening and time publicly in adoration at the altar. We can learn much from Abraham's example.

Read Genesis 12:1–4. What did God tell Abraham to do? (v. 1)

Was this a test? Of what?

Could it be said that the call of God is always some sort of testing? Explain. Personalize.

What was God's promise to Abraham? (v. 3)

What is the spiritual implication for us in reading verse 4?

 KINGDOM EXTRA

Faith. Abraham's ability to lead was tested in three areas of faith: 1) Faith to risk (Gen. 12:1–5): A wealthy man, Abraham risked all to follow God. The godly leader is willing to risk everything on God's faithfulness, and venture into the unknown. 2) Faith to trust (17:1–27): Abraham and Sarah were long past the age of child-bearing. The godly leader does not rely on facts alone, but goes beyond facts to faith. 3) Faith to surrender (22:1–19). Abraham knew the sacrifice of his son would destroy any hope of fulfilling God's promise that he would father many nations. The godly leader is willing to sacrifice all things precious in order to please God.[1]

 FAITH ALIVE

Turn now to Genesis 13:1–4. Here read how Abraham returned to an altar and worshiped the Lord. Although he demonstrated a seriousness about God's call, evidenced in his willingness to risk, he was also mindful of his continual need for God. Even though God calls and we choose to obey, we still may need regular times of refreshing, retooling, thereby renewing our spirit and reframing our perspective.

What happened before this "altar" encounter?

What do you see as significant to Abraham's meeting God at this particular time?

An altar is symbolic. At an Old Testament altar, persons reflected about God, dialogued with God, and received strength from God to continue the task. At the altar, Abraham could be honest and transparent, consequently opening himself to receive sustenance from the Lord. "Without regular worship, it is difficult to remember what God desires and even more difficult to obey."[5]

Have you ever built an altar to the Lord, figuratively speaking? Reflect on its significance.

Read Genesis 13:12–18.

What happened to Abraham at an altar next?

What was the spiritual climate of the times?

What did God say to Abraham?

How can this encounter be applied to your life?

Connect what happened at the two altars in this chapter.

Now read Genesis 17:1–11. Years had passed and Abraham's growth in God was deep and real. What did God say to Abraham when he was 90 years old? (v. 1)

Is His admonition any different for us? What does this mean to your understanding?

Because Abraham was serious about the call of God, he obeyed God. What did God establish with him? (v. 7)

WORD WEALTH

Covenant, *berit.* A covenant, compact, pledge, treaty, agreement. This is one of the most theologically important words in the Bible, appearing more than 250 times in the Old Testament. A *berit* may be made between individuals, between a king and his people, or by God with His people. Here God's irrevocable pledge is that He will be God to Abraham and his descendants *forever.* The greatest provision of the Abrahamic covenant, this is the foundation stone of Israel's eternal relationship to God, a truth affirmed by David (2 Sam. 7:24), by the Lord Himself (Jer. 33:24–26), and by Paul (Rom. 9:4; 11:2, 29). All other Bible promises are based on this one.[o]

What was Abraham to gain from his agreement with God? (vv. 6–10)

List several blessings you receive or inherit from being a member of God's family?

Circumcision was a highly significant part of the covenant between God and Abraham (vv. 10, 11). It has symbolic and spiritual implications for modern worshipers as well. Carefully read the "Behind the Scenes" entry below.

BEHIND THE SCENES

Circumcision's Significance. The act of circumcision was required as a sign of the covenant previously established with Abraham. This was not a new covenant but an external sign that Abraham and his descendants were to execute to show that they were God's covenant people. The fact that this was performed upon the male reproductive organ had at least a twofold significance: 1) the cutting away of the foreskin spoke of the cutting away of fleshly dependence, and 2) their hope for the future posterity and prosperity was not to rest upon their own ability. Circumcision was a statement that confidence was being placed in the promise of God and His faithfulness rather than in their own flesh.[7]

Reflect:

• How might you be manifesting fleshly dependence?

• What would it mean for you to become more God-dependent in those areas?

DAVID, THE KING OF ISRAEL

David, another man serious about God's call, subsequently arranged his life accordingly and his worship of God shaped his life. The Book of Psalms is laden with rich examples of David's desire to please God, once he grasped God's call to worship and to serve Him. His pursuit of God at an intimate dimension is very instructive.

Read the following Scripture texts, remembering the admonishment of James 1:22 as a wise precaution that we not merely *study,* but that we be *shaped.* What does James say?

Now, read Psalm 5:1–3 and let's capture the heart of David.

What is the difference between words and meditation? (v. 1)

Describe your viewpoint on why David appeals to God to bring both words and meditations under review.

When does David come with prayer and worship?

What distinct value do you see in this timing?

 KINGDOM EXTRA

Patterns in Prayer and Spiritual Breakthrough. In [Psalm 5:1–3] David builds a case for consistency and order in daily prayer. The repetition of the phrase "in the morning" justifies an alternate translation: "morning by morning." Also significant is the psalmist's selection of the Hebrew word *'arak* ("direct") in his declaration that he would "direct" his petitions to God daily. *'Arak* is most frequently used in Moses' writings in reference to the priests "setting in order" the sacrifices to be brought to the Lord each day (Ex. 40:4); also to describe an army being "set in array" in preparation for battle (Judg. 20:20–22). Such usage indicates an "ordered strategy" has been prepared for battle. These definitions connote the thought that David's "direct" prayer speaks of a well-thought-out order to his prayers, a daily prayer strategy with purpose and meaning.[8]

Read Psalm 9:1, 2, 13, 14.

David _____ with his whole heart (v. 1). How would you imagine that being exercised?

He _____ in the Lord. He _____ _____to His name (v. 2). How would you do this on a morning-to-morning basis?

For what does David ask? (v. 13)

What is his motive? (v. 14)

Read Psalm 16:1, 2. When does David trust?

Quote David's statement of humility.

How is humility significant in any relationship, but especially in our communion with God Almighty?

Read Psalm 23. List the verbs used in this beloved Psalm to describe our Shepherd's dealings with those who follow Him in worshipful obedience.

How does each apply to your life presently?

Another key to David's worship life was his readiness to confess and forsake sin. Read Psalm 51:1–5, 10–13 for more on this trait of the serious seeker.

Those who respond to the call of God are serious about His directive(s). Find scriptural support for how Abraham and David each did the following:

	Abraham	David
• repented when wrong	_____	_____
• moved when told	_____	_____
• prayed early in the morning	_____	_____
• built altars	_____	_____
• sang	_____	_____
• worshiped	_____	_____
• taught their children godly principles	_____	_____
• prioritized all of life around God's plan	_____	_____

Their worship birthed a heritage from which we glean today. Their obedience to God's call establishes a model. Abraham was so successful in developing obedience that God called him "my friend" and David was called "the man after God's own heart." As John Perkins has said, "Authentic faith is faith that obeys."⁹ These two giants *grew* that size from a posture on their knees . . . in worship!

GIDEON: TEACHABLE WHEN CALLED

Another aspect inherent in being willing to follow God's call is the quality of teachableness. Those who are teachable will grow in spiritual maturity. They learn from their mistakes, and thereby gain insight into life's challenges. However, being teachable connotes more than a willingness to learn. It requires a state of humility, which is rare. Those who are teachable take God more seriously than they take themselves. They are not prideful or stubborn. They recognize God's infinite capacity to speak through others. Teachable persons respect all of humanity. They can learn from the aged and the young. To garner a spirit of teachableness is of lifetime value, prohibiting pride as experiences accrue and blessing increases.

Gideon lacked faith but was willing to learn to trust God. His teachable spirit created the path for a more preferable future.

Read Judges 6:11–24. Recount the story of Gideon's call in key excerpts and list below:

v. 12:

v. 15:

v. 16:

v. 17:

v. 19:

vv. 22–24:

 KINGDOM EXTRA

Humility. Gideon demonstrates seven traits of godly leadership: 1) unwillingness to lead unless God calls (Judg. 6:36–40); 2) dependence on God at every turn (7:1–8); 3) willingness to turn faith into action (6:25–27; 7:15–22); 4) willingness to use the gifts God had given him to lead others. He told the 300 who stuck with him to watch him and follow his example (7:17); 5) he gave God glory before and after his victory (7:15; 8:3, 23); 6) he humbly gave others credit that belonged to him (8:1–3); 7) he refused to establish a dynasty after he had fulfilled God's charge (8:22, 23).[10]

Gideon accomplished great feats for God after hearing God's call and responding positively. Remember, though, that Gideon questioned the call initially. All he needed was proof and reassurance. Once convinced, he moved courageously and decisively. Gideon is even recorded in Hebrews 11:32 as a leader who, through remaining teachable:

- grew in faith and subdued kingdoms
- out of weakness was made strong
- became valiant in battle

Which of Gideon's fears can you see in yourself?

What of Gideon's faith would you pray to receive—now?

NOW ADD CHILDLIKENESS

Closely associated with the quality of being teachable is the attribute of childlikeness. It is a facet of character development in the kingdom of God. Childlikeness is a willing dependency upon our heavenly Father, who obviously knows what is best for us. Therefore, when He calls, His children listen carefully. For, "a child in arms has neither social influence nor personal strength upon which to rely."[11] Becoming childlike necessitates a dying to the flesh. We give up our right toward self-governance. A childlike spirit is a precious trait for a believer to develop. God is moved by childlike faith.

Read Matthew 18:1–5. What does Jesus say about humility? (v. 4)

Reflect on the relationship between a parent and young child. When the parent calls, the child responds. How is this scenario relevant to our lives as believers desirous of a call from God?

How can a believer formulate humility into his or her life-style?

IN SUM

Being willing to embrace the call of God to worship and serve Him presupposes our being sensitive, serious, and teachable and possessed of a childlike spirit.

As a worship expression, take time now to sing:

> *All to Jesus I surrender,*
> *All to Him I freely give.*
> *I will ever love and thank Him,*
> *In His presence daily live;*
> *I surrender all . . .*
> Judson W. Van deVenter

1. *Spirit-Filled Life Bible* (Nashville, TN: Thomas Nelson Publishers, 1991), 1567, "Truth-in-Action through the Synoptic Gospels."

2. Ibid., 1508, "Kingdom Dynamics: Faithful Mother: Obedient Disciple (Mary)."

3. Max Lucado, *And the Angels Were Silent: The Final Week of Jesus* (Questar Publishers, Multnomah Books, 1992), 51.

4. *Spirit-Filled Life Bible*, 24, "Kingdom Dynamics: Faith."

5. New Testament Life Application Notes and Bible Helps © 1986 owned by assignment to Tyndale House Publishers, Inc. *Life Application Bible* © 1988, 1989, 1990, 1991 by Tyndale House Publishers, Inc., Wheaton, IL 60189. Used by permission. All rights reserved. *Life Application* is a registered trademark of Tyndale House Publishers, Inc.

6. *Spirit-Filled Life Bible*, 29, "Word Wealth: 17:7 covenant."

7. Ibid., "Kingdom Dynamics: Circumcision's Significance."

8. Ibid., 756, "Kingdom Dynamics: Patterns in Prayer and Spiritual Breakthrough."

9. From: *Practical Christianity*, p. 196. Compiled and edited by LaVonne Neff, Ron Beers, Bruce Barton, Linda Taylor, Dave Veerman, and Jim Galvin. © 1987 by Youth for Christ/USA. Used by permission of Tyndale House Publishers, Inc. All rights reserved.

10. Ibid., 354, "Kingdom Dynamics: Humility."

11. *The Communicator's Commentary*, Vol. 2; Mark (206) by Dr. David L. McKenna; gen. ed. Lloyd J. Ogilvie. Copyright 1982, Word Inc., Dallas, TX. Used with permission.

Lesson 3/The Command to Worship

Worship is central to our faith in Christ. The implications for the true disciple are all-encompassing, for worship is more than an event on Sunday morning—it becomes a life-style. True worship will spill over into the week—informing choices, determining perspectives, offering a cup of cold water, loving the unlovely, practicing fidelity, and a cluster of other wholesome actions and attitudes. These attributes may, in fact, run counter to our culture. For the Christian who pursues the worship of a holy God will pursue a holy life-style as a natural by-product.

In his writing Graham Kendrick has linked "worship" and "discipline," two words most people probably seldom think of together.[1] Yet to embrace the essence of the biblical standard in its clearest form, one must practice discipline in the pursuit of worshiping God. As human beings, we naturally are fallible. Whenever we sin, our God is holy and sinless. Therefore, we wisely and regularly seek forgiveness in order to commune with Him. This is a discipline. As we mature, overt sin falls away, but we sensitively will still take regular inventory of the inner man to deter anything that interferes with our worship experience.

What are examples of potential problems we need vigilantly to monitor, in pursuit of a biblical, worship-based life-style? Consider, for example, unforgiveness, complaining, gossiping, omitting one's tithe, prayerlessness, and unwholesome thought life.

The Bible says, "God is Spirit, and those who worship Him must worship in spirit and truth" (John 4:24). How can I assert my seriousness about worshiping our Lord "in truth" by being truthful regarding sin I discover in my heart?

Let's decide now to be rid of such hindrances. Let us seek forgiveness and, where necessary, make restitution.

DEFINING WORSHIP

Worship is an event and a process.

In the worship event, we gather to honor and revere Christ through certain patterns and traditions. Robert Webber writes, "The focus of worship is not human experience, not a lecture, nor entertainment, but Jesus Christ—his life, death and resurrection."[2] Bob Sorge complements that thought, stating, "The goal for our worship should be that we come to the point when we do not see anyone or anything around us, but we become totally taken up with God. This is the supreme goal of worship: to see only the Lord."[3] That is the worship event.

Then, with the event, there is the worship process. Simply stated, this refers to our discipleship—the maturation sequence in which we move from self-centeredness to Christ-centeredness. LaMar Boschman writes, "We must develop a life of worship, living in His presence, not just visiting on weekends. The Lord is looking for worshipers, not just worship."[4]

Having established our objective—to become worshipers—let's investigate scriptural commands on the theme, taking as our key Psalm 113:3, "From the rising of the sun to its going down, the LORD's name *is* to be praised." These words encapsulate worship, both as an event and a process.

COMMANDS TO WORSHIP

We are commanded in Scripture to worship. There is no optional clause available in which the command may be modified. Simply follow the instructions. Those are our marching orders as Spirit-filled believers.

Read 2 Kings 17:24–39. What was the Lord's charge and why was it given? (vv. 34, 35)

What is the setting in which this was given? (vv. 24–31)

What is the astounding double-mindedness mentioned? (vv. 32, 33)

What is commanded about other gods? (v. 35)

Why does God claim this right to allegiance? (v. 36)

What specific directives are given and what reward is promised? (vv. 37–39)

Read Psalm 29:1, 2 and learn Spirit-filled steps to dynamic devotions. Express the meaning of these commands in your own words. Elaborate.

What are ways you can give "glory" to the Lord as a worshiper? as a witness? as a servant?

What do you think the Bible means by "the beauty of holiness"? (v. 2)

To properly inform your answer, consider the following word studies from the *Spirit-Filled Life Bible.*

 WORD WEALTH

Holy, *qadosh.* Set apart, dedicated to sacred purposes; holy, sacred, clean, morally or ceremonially pure. The verb *qadash* means "to set apart something or someone for holy purposes." Holiness is separation from everything profane and defiling; and at the same time, it is dedication to everything holy and pure. People or even objects, such as anointing oil or vessels, may be considered holy to the Lord (Ex. 30:25; Jer. 2:3; Zech. 14:20, 21). Leviticus stresses "holy" and "holiness" most thoroughly. Leviticus 10:10 shows that God desired that the priests be able to distinguish "holy" and "unholy" and teach Israel to do likewise. God is entirely holy in His nature, motives, thoughts, words, and deeds so that He is called *Qadosh,* "the Holy One" or *Qedosh Yisrael,* "the Holy One of Israel." Thus [Leviticus] 19:2 can say, "You shall be *qedoshim* [holy ones] for I . . . *am* holy."[5]

Holiness, *hagiosune.* See 1 Thessalonians 3:13. The process, quality, and condition of a holy disposition and the quality of holiness in personal conduct. It is the principle that separates the believer from the world. *Hagiosune* consecrates us to God's service both in soul and in body, finding fulfillment in moral dedication and a life commitment to purity. It causes every component of our character to stand God's inspection and meet His approval.[6]

God wants us to see the "beauty" that is not only inherent in His character and completeness, but through our worship to allow Him to pour the same into us. His "holiness" is ready to be infused into the humble worshiper who comes openly to Him.

Read Psalm 95:1–7. What are we told to do? (v. 1) Compare this with other commandments to sing found in Psalms 30:4; 33:1–3; 98:1; 147:1, 7 and note distinctive traits of each call "to sing."

In the light of these calls, what attitudes should we cultivate as we come before Him in song, and what might we expect as we do?

 WORD WEALTH

Thanksgiving, *todah.* Thanks, thanksgiving, adoration, praise. This word is derived from the verb *yadah,* "to give thanks, to praise." The root of *yadah* is *yad,* "hand." Thus, to thank or praise God is "to lift or extend one's hands" in thanks to Him. *Todah* appears more than thirty times in the Old Testament, a dozen of these in the Psalms (50:23; 100:4). *Todah* is translated "sacrifice of praise" in Jeremiah 33:11.[7]

Where might you focus your thanks when you pray? when you attend a worship service? when you face a trial or need? where you have gained a victory or experienced an answer to prayer?

How can we keep a spirit of thanksgiving fresh and relevant?

What are we told to do in Psalm 95:6–8?

Why do you think the physical expression directed is called for? (v. 6)

Outline the first three phrases in verse 7 and express the thought behind each as a call to worship.

What can be avoided with this order of worship? (v. 8)

Read Psalm 99:1–5. The "reign" of the Lord focuses us on His kingdom power and its availability to our present moment. Reflect on Psalm 99:1–5, and note:

What appropriate responses are mentioned to the reality of God's reign? (vv. 1–3)

What action will God take in the midst of, or in behalf of, such worship and worshipers? (v. 4)

What two verbs are listed in verse 5? Look in your concordance and list three other scriptural references where each verb is used.

    WORD WEALTH

Worship, *shachah*. To bow, to stoop; to bow down before someone as an act of submission or reverence; to worship; to fall or bow down when paying homage to God. The primary meaning is "to make oneself low." In Psalm 99:5, *shachah* is used in contrast to exaltation: exalt the Lord (lift Him up high) and worship (bow yourselves down low before Him) at the place of His feet.[8]

Worship is attitudinal. Worship is also physical. There are appropriate times to sing, bow, kneel, stand, clap, shout, or simply celebrate. As someone has said, "There are times for 'high church' (ceremony) and times to 'have church' (celebration)!"

Psalm 100:1–5 provides keys to practicing dynamic praise in God's presence.

What *attitudes* should accompany sincere worship and praise? (cf. vv. 1, 2, 4)

What *actions* express sincere worship and praise? (cf. vv. 1, 2, 4)

Are these actions of worship more verbal or physical? Does this surprise you?

WORD WEALTH

Serve, *'abad*. To work for, serve, do labor for someone; to be a servant; to worship. From this verbal root comes *'ebed*, "servant," "slave," or "laborer." "Servant" is generally someone who acts at the bidding of a superior. The most significant bearer of this designation is the messianic "Servant of the Lord" in Isaiah. *'Abad* appears in several names, among which are Obed-Edom ("Servant of Edom"), Abed-Nego ("Servant of Nego"), and Obadiah ("Servant of Yah"). Psalm 35:27 illustrates how much God values and is kindly disposed to His servants. Unlike human overlords and masters, God is deeply concerned with the total well-being of each of His servants.[9]

WORD WEALTH

Praise, *tehillah*. A celebration, a lauding of someone praiseworthy; the praise or exaltation of God; praises, songs of admiration. The noun *tehillah* comes from the verb *halal*, which means "to praise, celebrate, and laud." The Hebrew title of the Book of Psalms is *Tehillim,* literally the Book of Praises.[10]

Psalm 145 covers nearly every aspect of verbal praise. How many words connected with verbal praise can you find and list from verses 1–21?

 WORD WEALTH

Bless, *barach.* To bless, to salute, congratulate, thank, praise; to kneel down. *Barach* is the root word from which *baruch* ("blessed one") and *barachah* ("blessing") are derived. *Berech,* "knee," is probably the source of those words. In Old Testament times, one got down on his knees when preparing to speak or receive words of blessing, whether to God in heaven, or to the king on his throne. From God's side, He is the Blesser, the One who gives the capacity for living a full, rich life. The first action of God the Creator to the newly created man and woman was to bless them (Gen. 1:28). The Aaronic Benediction (Num. 6:22–27) epitomizes God's promise of blessing to His people. In Jewish worship, God is frequently called *ha-Qodesh, baruch hu,* or literally, "the Holy One, blessed is He!"[11]

Perceiving worship as a process, list ways you can bless the Lord in your workday environment, at home, and in your personal quiet time. (A chart is provided for your convenience.)

Work Environment	At Home	In Quiet Time
1.	1.	1.
2.	2.	2.
3.	3.	3.

CHARACTERISTICS OF AUTHENTIC WORSHIP

Anyone who follows the biblical commands to worship will soon display in worship biblical characteristics that are discernable. These characteristics include:

- The Worship of God Alone
- The Love of God with All of One's Heart
- A Dependency on the Holy Spirit[12]
- A Focus on Glorious Praise
- A Balancing of Seriousness with Enthusiasm
- An Avoidance of Sin
- A Concentration on Unity and Order[13]

Let's consider each characteristic by reviewing related scriptural references.

The Worship of God Alone

Read Exodus 20:3–5. Why did God demand exclusive loyalty?

Why did God forbid creating any image of Him?

Is there anything or anyone in your life which or who commands more of your loyalty, time, or attention than God does?

If yes, you should reevaluate your behavior and relationship. I suggest a pastoral consultation if you are unsure or ambivalent.

The Love of God with All of One's Heart

Read Deuteronomy 6:4–9. What do you think are the present-day implications of each facet of this passage?

True biblical worship is a matter of process—to be lived out in the routine of our lives. How is this confirmed in verses 7–9?

How can loving God with all your heart be demonstrated in your life and before your family and friends?

A Dependency on the Holy Spirit

Read Philippians 3:3 (note John 4:24 as well). What does it mean to worship God "in the Spirit"? (See *Spirit-Filled Life Bible*, 1805, note on 3:3.)

How are you becoming increasingly sensitive to the Spirit in your life as a worshiper?

In what ways do you find you have to resist your "flesh" in your efforts to "worship God in the Spirit"?

A Focus on Glorious Praise

Read Psalm 66:1–4. List the commands given in verses 1 and 2.

Have you ever literally shouted out praises to God? What were the circumstances? How did you feel?

Check a dictionary to be sure you understand the meaning of the word "glory." Then write four to six synonyms for "glory" or "glorious."

How can we make our praises "glorious" to God?

A Balancing of Seriousness with Enthusiasm

Read 1 Chronicles 13:6–12. Who drove the cart carrying the ark of God? (v. 7)

What seems to be the significance of listing their names and the manner in which they transported the ark?

 FAITH ALIVE

In this juxtapositioning of verses 7 and 8, we may observe the seriousness with which the ark was transported, as well as a joyous musical celebration, which followed. So, in our worship experiences, there are vivid contrasts, which are to be enjoyed—the receiving of the elements of communion and a heartfelt, passionate gospel song following, or the reading of a scripture with fiery preaching subsequently. Believers throughout the centuries have managed a balance between the serious and the enthusiastic—between "intimacy and theater."[14]

How do you know David worshiped God with enthusiasm? (see v. 8 and 15:29)

How would you describe the degree to which you "enjoy" worshiping God?

Are you more inclined to be one who worships "with all [his] might" or one who watches and seeks to steady the ark?

AT A GLANCE

Truth 1 Chronicles Teaches	Action 1 Chronicles Invites
Keys to Wise Living Wisdom counsels us that God's ways are higher than our ways and His thoughts than our thoughts. He knows the best way to do His work.	**Do not undertake** to do God's work in your own way. **Be warned** that employing human wisdom to accomplish God's work can result in frightening consequences.[15]

An Avoidance of Sin

Read Jeremiah 7:8–16. This passage delineates seven things that will hinder the hand of God. List them:

1.

2.

3.

4.

5.

6.

7.

Now list the three things the Lord requires of us, as found in Micah 6:8.

1.

2.

3.

Now compare the two lists above and see what you notice. Be specific and practical in thinking through their meaning to your experience. What observations would you make?

Can we sincerely worship God and be committed to practicing or tolerating sin in our lives at the same time? Why?

A Concentration on Unity and Order

Read 1 Corinthians 14:26, 33, 40. Contrast your enjoyment of a public meeting that is peacefully conducted with one in which chaos and confusion dominate.

What aspects of ministry are listed from a typical Christian worship service in Corinth?

What are to be the perceived results from ministry by various members of the body of Christ in public worship services?

 FAITH ALIVE

Self-control, mutual respect, and attention to organizational detail liberate a church service to realize ministry and fulfill spiritual objectives. Let's paradigm shift for a moment: when the fans remain in their seats and off the field, a baseball game can transpire effectively. When we obey the traffic laws, we increase our chances of avoiding accidents and arriving safely at our destination. When the audience holds their applause until the end of a symphony, one can appreciate the contrasts of each movement. There is profound merit in conducting any public gathering decently and in order. Laws and mores set up limits. Limits liberate participants from danger, so they may focus productively on the task at hand.

LET'S BUILD AN ALTAR

What we have done is take "altar-building" steps through our study. As the patriarchs of the Old Testament frequently built an altar in order to worship the Lord and remember His faithfulness, see how we are preparing to do the same—to figuratively construct an altar. As a technique for review think this through with me.

First, in biblical times, an appropriate spot would be chosen and the brush and debris would be cleared away. Likewise, as we have prepared for effective worship, we first have had to clear away any hindrances to worship. (Review your list.)

Second, the prophets would lay the stones in a logical sequence or order. This signifies our bringing definition to worship. Recall how we have done that.

- Worship is an event and a process.
- The focus of worship is Jesus Christ—His life, death, and resurrection.
- The goal of worship is to become totally centered on the Lord.
- The worship process refers to daily discipleship.
- We must develop a worship life-style (that is, throughout the week), not only being "weekend worshipers."

Third, in the Old Testament, worshipers would find an animal that was perfect in every way. Because the Old Testament code was very specific, they would prepare the sacrifice exactly according to regulation. In analogy, this could refer to our obeying the scriptural commands regarding worship. Worship of a holy God must be accomplished according to biblical mandates. (Again, review the scriptures we've studied on our "call" to worship.)

Finally, a sacrifice was offered. And so today we offer the sacrifice of praise, which has certain identifiable characteristics. These together "build an altar":

- The Worship of God Alone
- The Love of God with All of One's Heart
- A Dependency on the Holy Spirit
- A Focus on Glorious Praise
- A Balancing of Seriousness with Enthusiasm
- An Avoidance of Sin
- A Concentration on Unity and Order

IN SUM

Reflecting on the call to worship, informed by the command to worship, let's embrace the lyric . . .

There's a call—
It's coming from the mountain,
To one and all—
There's a call—
A call to every tribe and nation.
Worship Him—
The Lamb who sits upon the throne.
—Don Moen[16]

1. Graham Kendrick, *Learning to Worship as a Way of Life* (Minneapolis, MN: Bethany House Publishers, 1984), 182.

2. Robert Webber, *Worship Is a Verb* (Waco, TX: Word Books, Publishers, 1985), 11.

3. Bob Sorge, *Exploring Worship* (New Wilmington, PA: Son Rise Publishing and Distributing Co., 1987), 30.

4. LaMar Boschman, "Worship Forum" (*The Psalmist*, June/July 1992, Vol. 7, No. 3), 9.

5. *Spirit-Filled Life Bible* (Nashville, TN: Thomas Nelson Publishers, 1991), 171, "Word Wealth: 19:2 holy."

6. Ibid., 1829, "Word Wealth: 3:13 holiness."

7. Ibid., 836, "Word Wealth: 95:2 thanksgiving."

8. Ibid., 838, "Word Wealth: 99:5 worship."

9. Ibid., 839, "Word Wealth: 100:2 serve."

10. Ibid., "Word Wealth: 100:4 praise."

11. Ibid., 875, "Word Wealth: 145:2 bless."

12. *The NIV Topical Study Bible.* Copyright © 1989 by The Zondervan Corporation. Used by permission. All rights reserved.

13. New Testament Life Application Notes and Bible Helps © 1986 owned by assignment to Tyndale House Publishers, Inc. *Life Application Bible* © 1988, 1989, 1990, 1991 by Tyndale House Publishers, Inc., Wheaton, IL 60189. Used by permission. All rights reserved. *Life Application* is a registered trademark of Tyndale House Publishers, Inc.

14. Robert Webber, "From Jesus to Willow Creek" (*Discipleship Journal*, July/August 1992. Issue 70), 47.

15. *Spirit-Filled Life Bible,* 607, "Truth-in-Action through 1 Chronicles."

16. From "Come and Worship," by Don Moen © 1988 Integrity Hosanna/Music.

Lesson 4/And Your Response?

"Worship is a verb."[1] It presupposes action. In our pilgrimage toward an abundant, power-filled, and victorious Christian life, we have to prioritize the activity of worship. The word commands us to do so. Our joyous task is to obey—to be available.

Our forthcoming lessons will impart practical tools enabling participation in the worship event, as on Sundays, as well as empowering the process of worship through meaningful devotional life techniques during the week. Our goal: to be worshipers all week, not just in the Sunday sanctuary.

However, the focus of this lesson is introspective, for before we can proceed in more practical ways, we must elect to respond to Jesus' call as disciples. Jesus spoke of a disciple as being one who would "take up His cross daily, and follow . . ." (Luke 9:23). How must—how can I—respond to Jesus and open the way to worship as a valid, daily part of my experience? Will you respond to His call to *follow*? This means more than merely to "believe"; it means to *heed* and move in His ways. It is Jesus who has admonished us to "count the cost" (Luke 14:28–33) of discipleship. What two ideas does He relate to this?

What "building" (relationships, goals, and so on) do you envision in your life?

What battles do you face?

Clearly, discipleship unto worship is a practical call. Let's investigate the opportunity and cost for those who commit to a life of worship.

Specifically, we will study the Scripture from the perspective of analyzing the:

- Promises of those who are faithful to God
- Promises of those who are faithful to worship God
- Promises of those who are obedient to God
- Qualities that may move the hand of God on our behalf

Reflecting on these things will bring an informed basis for your decision: "Will I respond?"

THOSE FAITHFUL TO GOD

Adopting an attitude or mind-set to embrace faithfulness as a life-style is a tall order. Faithful persons are committed persons. Faithful persons are loyal persons. Faithful persons are responsible persons. Their word is a bond. A faithful person will choose to forgo distractions for the prescribed goal. They are not dissuaded by "wind or weather," by personalities, by fatigue, or other distractions. That is why God rewards faithfulness so highly—why He places such a premium on faithfulness in our pursuit of heaven. Do you recall the parable of the talents?

Read Matt. 25:14–30. What did the Lord say to the servant who was given five talents? (v. 21)

Over what was he faithful? (v. 21)

What were his two rewards? (v. 21)

1.

2.

How would you apply this lesson to your present? to your foreseeable future?

Read Psalm 31:23, 24. What verb does this Psalm use to actualize what God does for faithful persons? (v. 23) What prompts this? What benefits can you imagine it suggests?

Faithful reader, write out verse 24. What do you think a "strengthened heart" refers to?

Note the rewards of faithfulness in worship and service: (a) promotion (He will make you "ruler" over many things), and (b) mental health (you'll be of good courage and possess a strong heart).

Contrast the reward of faithfulness in Proverbs 28:20 with the loss of self-serving ways.

What does Revelation 2:10 show as the ultimate blessing for faithfulness?

What do you think this refers to? Is it only future? How might it apply to the present?

Let's study some who were counted as "faithful" in the Bible.

Read Galatians 3:6 regarding <u>Abraham</u>.

Abraham was faithful to _____.

It was counted to him for _____.

How does such a reward apply to us today? (Rom. 4:3–5, 16)

Read Hebrews 3:5 regarding <u>Moses</u>.

Moses was faithful _____.

Since "house" refers to a person's God-intended arena of responsibility, how might this apply to you?

Read 2 Samuel 22:21–25 regarding <u>David</u>.

David _____ the ways of the Lord.
He did not _____ from His statutes.
David was _____ before Him.
He kept himself from _____.

David was faithful to remain pure, blameless. God rewarded him according to his _____ and _____ in His eyes. (v. 21)

How would you see each of these attributes advanced in your own heart, attitudes, and life?

Read Job 1:21, 22 and 2:9, 10 regarding Job.

Job was faithful in adversity.
He fell to the ground and worshiped, saying,
"The LORD_____ and the LORD has _____ away;
 Blessed be the _____ of the LORD."
And the Bible records,
"In all _____ , Job did not _____ nor
charge God with _____."

How would you compare your response to difficult circumstances?

What do you see as Job's source of ability to stand with such constancy?

FAITH ALIVE

The Bible records that Abraham, Moses, David, and Job were faithful to God. Each demonstrated a different connotation of the term "faith" as evidenced in his behavior, choices, and will. Each was rewarded positively. Are you struggling with adversity? Think of Job. You can make it, too! Are you plagued with guilt? Are you living in unconfessed sin? Think of David. He sinned. Yet he was quick to repent and seek forgiveness. And you and I can grow and increase in faithfulness as Abraham and Moses did. Right now, stop to praise God for that! You and I *can* rise as faithful worshipers! His grace and power promise it!

THOSE FAITHFUL TO WORSHIP GOD

It is clear that God responds to diligence. There is a profound correlation with those who worship Him faithfully and His blessings upon their life. We may deduce that God is conscientious about blessing those who worship Him.

Psalm 50:23 summarizes the fruit of praise.

What does praise accomplish?

What is the blessing stated for the person who orders his or her conduct aright?

Now, with this conclusion in view, read through the entire fiftieth psalm and write "praise phrases" in keeping with truths unfolded there. For example:

vv. 1–3 "Praise You, Lord, for You will come in triumph!"

vv. 4–6

v. 7

v. 12

v. 15

  FAITH ALIVE

Praise, the Road to Success. This whole chapter relates God's power, majesty, and glory, and is summed up in these closing verses, which apply to us as well as to the people of Israel. If we leave God out of our lives and live in rebellion, destruction follows. In contrast, the simple road to success is set forth: 1) Offer praise, and we glorify God. The focus of praise is directed toward God, but in His wisdom we are the ultimate beneficiaries. 2) We receive power to order our conduct; thus, our life-style comes into obedience to God. 3) Result: We receive a revelation (understanding)—that is, insight into God's salvation. Our praise becomes a vehicle for God to come to us and to minister through us.[2]

Read Psalm 63:3–5. What is better than life? (v. 3) Take time to divide this word and think through its generous intent.

As a result of praise and worship, David notes two benefits to the soul. List them (v. 5). What do you think these poetic terms mean?

a.

b.

FAITH ALIVE

Praise Releases Blessings and Satisfaction. This classic passage [Ps. 63:1–5] teaches how <u>expressed</u> praise releases the blessings of praise. Notice, this is not a silent prayer: "My <u>mouth</u> shall praise You with joyful lips." And look at the fruit: 1) "O God, You *are* my God" (affirmed relationship); 2) "Early will I seek You" (clear priorities); 3) "My soul thirsts . . . My flesh longs for You" (deep intensity); 4) "I have looked for You in the sanctuary, to see Your power and glory" (desire for corporate involvement); 5) "Because Your lovingkindness is better than life, my lips shall praise You" (appropriate gratitude); 6) <u>Result</u>: "My soul [the real me] shall be satisfied as with marrow and fatness" (personal needs met).[3]

Read Psalm 18:1–3. What attributes of God prompt David's statement, "The LORD *who is worthy* to be praised"?

What practical benefit does he note results from praise?

Read Psalm 7:14–17. Who "brings forth iniquity"? (v. 14) How?

Describe the psalmist's observations about the reversal of situations when he praises God instead of fearing the wicked. What does the psalmist do? (v. 17)

Apply this scenario to your own experience. Has worship ever served to preserve you in the face of an enemy or great adversity? Elaborate. Apply to your present circumstance.

Who was counted as faithful in their worship, as recorded in the Bible?

Read Daniel 6:1–21 regarding <u>Daniel</u>.

Daniel knelt down on his knees _____ times
that day and _____ and gave _____ before
his God, as was his _____ since early days.

As a result, God delivered him from the _____.

Read Daniel 3:1–29 regarding <u>Shadrach, Meshach, and
Abed-Nego</u>.

Having incurred the king's threats, Shadrach, Meshach,
and Abed-Nego boldly stated, ". . . Let it be known to you,
O king, that we do not serve your gods, nor will
we _____ the gold image which you have set up."

Consequently, God delivered them from the _____.

Read 2 Chronicles 20:1–30 regarding <u>Jehoshaphat</u>.

The imminent threat of an advancing horde of enemy sol-
diers sets the backdrop for Jehoshaphat's classic example of
proactivitiy—worship before the battle.
Following his courageous, faith-filled prayer, the Spirit of
the Lord fell upon the prophet Jahaziel. Record his word
(v. 15b): "Thus says the LORD to you:

Can you see a present possibility for applying this praise
principle personally? in your church? in your city? in your
nation?

The stories in the Word that recount God's faithfulness to
those who worshiped Him, even in the middle of struggle,
persecution, evil, or punishment, are multitudinous. Those
courageous enough to take worship seriously are always vin-
dicated—breakthrough follows! Believing "God shows no

partiality" (Acts 10:34), this is our inheritance, too, so let us respond with this wisdom in such circumstances.

THOSE OBEDIENT TO GOD

Simple obedience is anything but simple to do. The distractions of our culture, fueled by the demands of the world's rat race, can render us dizzy by the end of a day. Those who lack discernment, or the determination to follow Christ, may willfully walk their own way and be swept downstream in a flurry of temptations, situational ethics, and neon lights.

Following Christ in obedience—walking the straight and narrow—may be difficult at times, because you may feel lonely or isolated from the "in-crowd," but remember, dear one, you are not alone. The Lord promises:

- "I will never leave you nor forsake you." (Heb. 13:5b)
- "God sets the solitary in families." (Ps. 68:6)
- "Come to Me, all *you* who labor and are heavy laden, and I will give you rest." (Matt. 11:28)

God is with us. He is "Immanuel" (Matt. 1:23). Our obedience—(a) relative to withstanding peer pressure and its momentary allurement, (b) relative to obeying His commandments, (c) relative to our relationships and ethics in business practices, and (d) relative to our willingness to worship Jesus our Lord—carries great dividends of blessing beyond description. Let's study a few :

Read Isaiah 48:17, 18. What does the Lord teach you to do? (v. 17)

WORD WEALTH

Teaches, *lamad.* To instruct, train; prod, goad; teach; to cause someone to learn. The origin of the verb may be traced to the goading of cattle. Similarly, teaching and learning are attained through a great variety of goading, by memorable events, techniques, or lessons. From *lamad* comes *talmid, melammed,* and *Talmud,* being respectively, "scholar," "student," and the "Book of Rabbinic Learning."[4]

When we obey, what metaphors describe the resultant peace and righteousness? (v. 18)

God wants you to know this prosperity, peace, and righteousness. And praise is the pathway!

 FAITH ALIVE

Prosperity Is a Result. It is clear that God wants His children to prosper. How can anyone deny that? However, prosperity should not be the end in itself. It ought to be the result of a quality of life, commitment, dedication, and action that is in line with God's Word. [In 3 John 2] the word "prosper" (Greek *euodoo*) literally means "to help on the road" or "succeed in reaching." It clearly implies that divine prosperity is not a momentary, passing phenomenon, but rather it is an ongoing, progressing state of success and well-being. It is intended for every area of our lives: the spiritual, the physical and emotional, and the material. However, God does not want us to unduly emphasize any one area. We must maintain a balance.[5]

Read 1 Kings 3:14. What is the promise God made to Solomon?

What was Solomon's responsibility before the promise was manifested?

_____ in My ways,

_____ My statutes,

and My _____ .

How would you apply this triple directive to your life?

Read Deuteronomy 5:33. In addition to the promise of life, it is qualified,

"*that it may be*_____ with you,

and *that* you may _____ *your* days in

the land which you _____ ."

How would you relate this promise of a more preferable future to both emotional and financial stability?

Read Job 36:11. What are the conditions to the promises of God's goodness?

Consider what various types of "prosperity" could be intended in this verse:

Read Psalm 84:11. The Lord is described as a _____

and _____. What does this connote to you?

From the upright, what will be withheld?

Read Proverbs 3:1, 2. What are the two conditions mentioned? (v. 1)

With conditions met, what is the divine blessing made available to us? (v. 2)

FAITH ALIVE

Who can put a price tag on peace? Lying down at night with a clear conscience, looking a client in the eye at the end of a business transaction, smiling at your spouse upon returning from a lengthy trip—knowing your conscience is not convicting—these are mere examples of the blessing of the Lord on those who follow the laws of Scripture in clear, purposeful obedience. Actually, the Bible articulates behavioral limitations for our benefit and not to be punitive. Sin breeds guilt. Guilt drives away peace, creating a vacuum of despair, disaster, and depression. But following the Word's light creates pathways to joy, serenity, and satisfaction.

Are you satisfied, guilt-free, at peace? If not, a prayer of forgiveness complemented by a new determination to be obedient to the Word, and evidenced by a resolution to worship, can cleanse your spirit and release joy and peace. It's a spiritual fact verfied by scientific investigation. Praise releases endorphins—proteins that bring positive physical and emotional responses.

Read Proverbs 16:7. The Lord makes whom to be at peace with you ? (v. 7b)

Whom would you perceive as "enemies," that is, as problematic or hostile people inhibiting your freedom? Would you like to stop quarreling? fearing? disliking? What is the spiritual antibiotic mentioned? (v. 7a)

List ways in which you feel you may "please" the Lord.

In what ways do you feel you are vulnerable to "displeasing" Him?

If you have listed ways which you know bring displeasure to God, and they are a part of your current life-style, why not pause in prayer now, before proceeding any further?

Seek forgiveness. In childlike faith, welcome and receive His blessing anew. He's ready to assist you to a walk in wholeness. Rely upon His grace to transform your understanding. Then watch for His peace to begin to be personified in the attitudes of your "enemies."

QUALITIES THAT MOVE GOD'S HAND

The Bible seems to assert that certain human commitments, attitudes, or attributes solicit God's attention. Consider these six as found in Scripture; six qualities that might be said to "move God's hand." They are obedience; a broken, contrite heart; fear (of the Lord); good works; faith; and trust (in the Lord).

Let's investigate these qualities which, if properly developed, reform behavior.

Obedience

Read 1 Samuel 15:22. Why is obedience better than sacrifice?

A broken, contrite heart

Read Psalm 51:17. Why does God value contrition?

Fear (of the Lord)

Read Psalm 103:17, 18. What does it mean to properly fear the Lord? (Read Isaiah 8:13 for further insight.)

Good works

Read Hebrews 13:16. List ways in which you may share your talents and treasure with your church community; your neighborhood community; in world missions.

Church		Neighborhood		World Missions	
Talent	Treasure	Talent	Treasure	Talent	Treasure

Faith

Read Hebrews 11:6. Define faith. (Consult a Bible dictionary.)

How are insurmountable obstacles or hindrances removed in our lives? (Read Mark 11:20–24.)

Apply to your life. Is your faith strong? In which areas? Is it weak? How can you be strengthened in your faith?

Trust (in the Lord)

Read Psalm 31:19 and Proverbs 3:5, 6. In what ways have you trusted in the Lord and received His blessing?

None of these "works" are suggested as means of salvation. That can't be done (Eph. 2:7, 8). However, living faith does manifest in works (James 2:20–26); and God rewards, that is, He works in response to such actions of believers.

 FAITH ALIVE

Intimacy and Spiritual Breakthrough. Two words in [Proverbs 3:5, 6] are especially significant—the words "ways" and "acknowledge." The word "ways" (Hebrew *derek*) means "a road, a course, or a mode of action." It suggests specific opportunities a person may encounter on a recurring basis. The most common "segment of opportunity" we experience regularly is each new day. It is as if this passage suggests that in all our "days" we should acknowledge God, and in so doing He will direct our paths.

Of equal significance is the word "acknowledge" (Hebrew *yada'*). Elsewhere *yada'* is translated "know," meaning to know by <u>observation</u>, <u>investigation</u>, <u>reflection</u>, or first-hand <u>experience</u>. But the highest level of *yada'* is in "direct, intimate contact." This refers to life-giving intimacy, as in marriage. Applied to a spiritual context, it suggests an intimacy with God in prayer that conceives and births blessings and victories. Joined to our Proverbs text [3:5, 6], we might conclude that if in all our "days" we maintain *yada'* (direct, intimate contact with God), God promises to direct our paths toward fruitful, life-begetting endeavors.[6]

IN SUM

This is a pivotal moment in our study. You have been confronted with the call to worship and the command to worship. The benefits have been articulated. The attributes which create favor with God Almighty—childlikeness, obedience, contrition, faith—have been delineated.

Child of God, will you respond? Recall that worship is an event and a process. The process of growing in Christlikeness, becoming a disciple, is daily. Ongoing. Steadfast. But don't miss the event that occurs weekly—the Sunday-to-Sunday celebration of Christ's resurrection, in church, with believers.

Busyness is a lame excuse to miss. Fatigue isn't even worth qualifying. So, . . .

> *"Slow down.*
> *If God commanded it, you need it.*
> *If Jesus modeled it, you need it.*
> *God still provides the manna.*
> *Trust Him.*
> *Take a day (each week) to say no to work*
> *and yes to worship."* [7]
>
> —Max Lucado

1. Robert E. Webber, *Worship Is a Verb* (Waco, TX: Word Books Publishers, 1985), 12.

2. *Spirit-Filled Life Bible* (Nashville, TN: Thomas Nelson Publishers, 1991), 798, "Kingdom Dynamics: Praise, the Road to Success."

3. Ibid., 805, 806, "Kingdom Dynamics: Praise Releases Blessings and Satisfaction."

4. Ibid., 1025, 1026, "Word Wealth: 48:17 teaches."

5. Ibid., 1941, "Kingdom Dynamics: Prosperity Is a Result."

6. Ibid., 888, 889, "Kingdom Dynamics: Intimacy and Spiritual Breakthrough."

7. Max Lucado, *And the Angels Were Silent: The Final Week of Jesus* (Questar Publishers, Multnomah Books, 1992), 43.

Lesson 5/Preparing for the Worship Service

I love adages—sayings that encapsulate motivational thought. Some are humorous. Some are haunting. One that often frames my day is this: "To fail to plan is to plan to fail." Planning is a healthy venture, pregnant with reciprocity, for planning affects both the present and the future. To plan is to set in motion a series of circumstances in an orderly fashion. Once ordered, the chances of success regardless of the venture in question, are obviously greater than if one failed to plan.

Planning works.

It is interesting for me, as a worship leader, to observe people's ability to transfer learning. Some people plan to worship, coming to church prepared. Others seem to be preoccupied and fail to realize the potential present in a service. For example, an individual who is commercially successful may approach regular church attendance casually. At work, they arrive early and are consummately prepared. They focus. They remain on task. Overtime is no problem. They may be overheard quipping, "Let's close the deal—no matter what it takes!" But church worship somehow becomes compartmentalized, shoved into a lesser category. Such an attitude may be summed up this way: "If I'm there, okay, but my priority—indeed, my identity—is my work." But wait. Ultimately, what *is* more important?

A job lasts for a season, a project for a day, while worship penetrates eternity each time we enter with praises and moves toward a life forever. To prepare for our worship experience is to grasp a truth—to enter into the New Testament concept of the royal priesthood of believers. Priests under the Old Testament economy *prepared*. Should New Testament priests do less? How do 1 Peter 2:5 and 9 describe us as believers? The answer settles our calling, so let us prepare for every priestly encounter. I maintain that successful, vibrant, and productive believers will plan to worship long before they arrive in the pew on Sunday morning. They will apply habits known to be productive to their life-style as disciples of Jesus. For example, what an employee learns from the work environment can be specifically applied. Beneath each of the following, make your application of sound work habits to the practice of your church worship:

1. Arrive at work on time.

2. Come to meetings prepared.

3. Speak articulately.

4. Defer to the supervisor.

5. Be cognizant of the needs of those with whom you work.

6. Give your full time, honestly, knowing it will be rewarded.

Let's examine the assumptions inherent in being a Spirit-filled, royal priest.

THE ROYAL PRIESTHOOD

Before Christ came to earth, Old Testament worshipers approached God through a priest of the Mosaic order. Fellowship with God and forgiveness of sin were tied to animal sacrifice. The laws regarding a congregant's behavior in the temple were specific, with awesome penalties for disobedience or neglect.

For example, read Numbers 3:10. Who was authorized for worship?

What was the punishment of an outsider presuming to attempt priestly duties?

Christ's death ended the necessity for the Old Testament priesthood. He restored the pathway for mankind to find forgiveness, fellowship, and an eternal relationship with God, for His blood served as a propitiation for our sins. Consequently, we may come into the presence of the heavenly Father directly. We no longer need the mediatorial role or advocacy of an earthly priest. In fact, now we are all called to function as priests, under Jesus Himself, our great one and only High Priest (Heb. 5:5–11).

Read 1 Peter 2:5, 9 again. List the four descriptions that apply to us as believers. (v. 9)
   •

   •

   •

   •

Whose praises are we to proclaim? (v. 9) Why?

Read Revelation 1:4–6. Who has made us kings and priests? What was the cost of this taking place?

Respond to its significance as you perceive your place in Christ
   —as a priest?

   —as a king?

KINGDOM EXTRA

Worship and Praise. In the opening of Revelation, John introduces himself as a brother and companion in the struggle we all face (v. 9). His words "in the kingdom and patience of Jesus Christ" point to the dual facts of Christ's present kingdom triumph and the ongoing presence of evil and warfare that exact the patience of the church in the kingdom advances among and through us. In prefacing the broad arenas of prophecy about to be unfolded, John addresses two very important <u>present</u> truths: 1) We, Christ's redeemed, are loved and are washed from our sins—a present state (v. 6). 2) We, through His glorious dominion, have been designated "kings and priests" to God—also a present calling. Thus, these dual offices give perspective on our authority and duty and how we most effectively may advance the kingdom of God.

First, we are said to be kings in the sense that under the King of kings we are the new breed—the reborn, to whom God has delegated authority to extend and administrate the powers of His rule. Of course, this involves faithful witness to the gospel in the power of the Spirit and loving service to humanity in the love of God. But it also involves confrontation with dark powers of hell, assertive prayer warfare, and an expectation of the miraculous works of God (2 Cor. 10:3–5; Eph. 6:10–20; 1 Cor. 2:4). However, this authority is only fully accomplished in the spirit of praiseful worship, as we exercise the office of "priests." Some translations read, "a kingdom of priests," which emphasizes that the rule is only effective when the priestly mission is faithfully attended. Worship is foundational to kingdom advance. The power of the believer before God's throne, worshiping the Lamb and exalting in the Holy Spirit of praise, is mightily confounding to the Adversary. See Exodus 19:5–7 and Psalm 22:3.[1]

As a royal (that is, kingly) priest, realizing that we can approach God directly, we now have certain responsibilities relative to the lives we lead.

Read John 14:6. What is the access route of our approach to God? (John 14:6; Rom. 5:2)

 WORD WEALTH

Foreigners, *paroikos.* From *para,* "beside," and *oikeo,* "to dwell"; hence, "dwelling near." The word came to denote an alien who dwells as a sojourner in a land without the rights of citizenship. The word describes Abraham and Moses, sojourners in a land not their own (Acts 7:6, 29), and the Christian who is traveling through this world as an alien whose citizenship and ultimate residence are in heaven (1 Pet. 2:11).[2]

Ephesians 2:19 contrasts "foreigner" and "citizen" with regard to our New Testament role as members of the Royal Priesthood. What does this mean to you?

Read Matthew 6:12 and Acts 17:30. Whose responsibility is it to seek forgiveness from God in prayer?

Who will signal our need to deal with sin? (Eph. 4:30)

Do we have to wait until a weekly worship service to seek forgiveness? Is it even wise to do so? Explain.

What should be done when sin taints our practice as believers? (1 John 1:9)

Romans 12:1, 2 is basically a call to worship. What are we told to present?

Why does this make personal purity desirable? (1 Cor. 6:19, 20)

What do you think it means to be "conformed to this world"? (Rom. 12:2)

How can worship bring about our transformation? (2 Cor. 3:17, 18)

In addition to presenting our bodies as a living sacrifice, what are we encouraged to bring as a sacrifice in worship? (Heb. 13:15, 16)

 FAITH ALIVE

The Sacrifice of Praise. Why is praising God a sacrifice? The word "sacrifice" (Greek *thusia*) comes from the root *thuo,* a verb meaning "to kill or slaughter for a purpose." Praise often requires that we "kill" our pride, fear, or sloth—anything that threatens to diminish or interfere with our worship of the Lord. We also discover here the basis of all our praise: the sacrifice of our Lord Jesus Christ. It is by Him, in Him, with Him, to Him, and for Him that we offer our sacrifice of praise to God. Praise will never be successfully hindered when we keep its focus on Him—the Founder and Completer of our salvation. His Cross, His Blood—His love gift of life and forgiveness to us—keep praise as a living sacrifice![3]

Verse 16 is a broad base plea to do good and share. Specifically, how can this verse be applied to your life each day? each Sunday?

EVERY BELIEVER'S RESPONSIBILITY

It is a new day, today, and vibrant worshipers are rising everywhere. Hearty worship flows from an understanding of the royal priesthood and a willingness to be focused, involved, and disciplined during the worship event. As Jack Hayford has said, today the Holy Spirit "is directing our appointment to priestly worship for the release of Kingdom advancement."[4] As we grow in our responsiveness in worship services, focusing on Jesus and His glory, we come into agreement. In an arena of focused, purposed agreement, the Lord is free to move, both *among* us and *on* our behalf. Worshipers, once renewed, soon are empowered to do exploits in the Savior's name.

We definitely have a role, though, to open this realm of possibility. We need to deny anything of a casual outlook and earnestly embrace our personal responsibility as priests in every service of worship we enter. We must plan in advance— arrive with a distinct frame of mind in place that will release our newly found role as a royal priest.

What is the role and responsibility of a believer, a congregant, each time a worship event is convened?

It's easy to articulate the role of a pastor or worship leader. The pastor comes to the worship service with a word from God for the people. He has prayed, studied, prepared, and is ready to nurture, admonish, edify, and/or increase vision. Then, the worship leader has also prepared. He or she, with the musicians, has arranged the flow of the songs, rehearsed and prepared through communion with the Lord. As a natural outgrowth of their preparation, the pastor and worship team are tuned already to enter into praise and worship. But what expectations might be made of the congregation—of you or me as we gather with the flock?

Are the responsibilities of the laity in worship to be any less rigorous, according to the Scripture? Are they to be any less prepared? Let's see.

Read Psalm 150. Who is commanded to praise? How are *all* participants enjoined to praise? Does this command include the clergy? the laity? young people? children?

Read Psalm 34:1. How often shall we praise and bless the Lord?

Elaborate on this verse, describing all it instructs by example—"I will."

What does all this mean to you? How can that understanding affect your worship in the weekly event?

 FAITH ALIVE

Graham Kendrick has observed that most of us let what we are feeling or experiencing influence the consistency of our expression of praise.[5] If we are happy, we praise freely. If we are downcast, we may exhibit a lack of focus, preoccupied with our woes. God is calling us to worship Him regardless of our emotional sensibility at any particular snapshot of time, and to become consistent in our worship life. Victorious worshipers are habitual worshipers. Victorious worshipers rise above circumstances. Victorious worshipers will to worship, not relying on an emotional stimulus, per se.

One way to become consistent in worship, every Sunday, is to prepare for the event. May I suggest the following:

1. Get a good night's rest before a worship event. Be careful of your stimulation on Saturday. Another adage—"Garbage in—garbage out." Who wants carnal images distracting one's focus on the Lord's day? Prepare your heart, as we've studied.
2. Pray in advance. Lift up the arms of your pastor. Invoke the Lord's presence and blessing upon the gathering.
3. Sanctify your drive. Instead of daydreaming or arguing, build an altar in your car. Play a worship tape. Involve the family in sentence prayers.

Determine to be a self-starter. Do not wait for someone else to stimulate your worship response—proactively assume responsibility for yourself. Isn't that the essence of maturity—to accept responsibility for your behavior? Motivation is a mind-set that eventually becomes a habit. Start this week!

Here are some thoughts to help cultivate a preworship mind-set. According to James 4:8–10, who begins the process in worship's approach?

What preparation is needed before we are lifted up by the Lord?

Practice the control of your thoughts. Worry is not advantageous in a believer's life. Read Philippians 4:6 and 1 Thessalonians 5:18. What do these verses say about controlling our thoughts? Be specific.

About what are you worried today? How can a worship mind-set reverse this posture?

Worship can so easily be distracted by worries. None of us want temporary issues to control our focus, while in a worship service. How can we change these patterns of thought? Read Romans 8:28–31, and note at least three reasons we can be encouraged in any circumstance:

So trust God! Worry only places you on a downward spiral. Worship eradicates that trend and reframes your perspective heavenward, where angels sing and prayers are answered.

Read Psalm 57:7. The psalmist realized God's potential to alter our circumstances on earth. Write your thinking about verse 7 in light of our newfound responsibilities as worshipers.

What deters distractions and keeps our focus on worship?

What is your best path to avoiding moodiness in your worship—sometimes enthusiastic, sometimes sullen—depending on our circumstances?

Is it possible to be cheerful and resilient, even if we do not feel like it? How? (Think of features of God's Person, His goodness to you, or His promises in the Word.) How can these thoughts establish a worship mind-set? List some of each of the three categories:

God's Person

God's goodness

God's promises

Let's take one last look at truth that can frame our mood and focus for worship.

Read 1 Peter 5:7. What does this verse communicate to you? (Examine the Word Wealth below before you respond.)

WORD WEALTH

Care, *merimna.* From *meiro,* "to divide," and *noos,* "the mind." The word denotes distractions, anxieties, burdens, and worries. *Merimna* means to be anxious beforehand about daily life. Such worry is unnecessary, because the Father's love provides for both our daily needs and our special needs.[6]

Philippians 4:6–8 also is helpful. How? Answer: For what are we to be anxious? What is to guard our hearts? What is the scriptural antidote for anxiety?

WORD WEALTH

Good report, *euphemos.* Compare "euphemism" and "euphemistic." A combination of *eu,* "well," and *pheme,* "a saying." *Euphemos* is speech that is gracious, auspicious, praiseworthy, and fair-sounding. It includes the avoidance of words of ill omen. An Old Testament counterpart is found in Proverbs 16:24: "Pleasant words *are like* a honeycomb, sweetness to the soul and health to the bones."[7]

Through the application of scriptural promises, believers are transformed. The Scripture renews the mind. Daily Bible study, meditation, memorization, and prayer of all types bolster the Christian to face, head-on, the challenges of the day. Be encouraged to inventory your quiet time. Are you balancing prayer with praise, meditation with memorization, supplication with solitude? Is your private time healthy?

COMMON HURDLES TO WORSHIP

Healthy people jump hurdles with ease. It's when we're out of shape that the hurdles seem higher and our energy decidedly lower. Giving time in God's presence daily will feed our energy for worship on Sunday. The worship "process" directly affects the worship "event."

Let's face it, biblical worship involves a real expenditure of energy. We may not feel like participating in worship—raising holy hands or standing for a hymn. That is precisely when we may need to, however. Determine to jump that hurdle of the flesh! Override the flesh's plea and walk in the Spirit. God will reward the earnest heart by renewing and refreshing both body and mind. Hallelujah! There *is* refreshing that comes when we are in God's presence. And it's priceless—truly priceless!

Not so priceless, however, are the three common hurdles to our freedom and effectiveness in the worship event. These are easily identified, having tempted us all to miss coming into God's presence. They are: pride, peer pressure[8], and preoccupation.

Pride

Who has ever met an arrogant person who was truly happy. A strange combination of criticism and sarcasm seemingly entwines their conversations, creating havoc interpersonally. A prideful person alienates easily. Pride is obviously distracting to worship.

A prideful attitude is exemplified in egocentric behavior. Often a prideful person will feel no particular need to enter into praise and worship experiences, doubtless feeling self-sufficient, self-satisfied. Pride objects to open, expressive praise or will employ it conversely to draw attention to oneself. The greatest danger is that pride overtakes one's heart incrementally. Pride is a subtle, yet growing, feeling that an accomplishment, position, or acquisition has been realized by the strength or wisdom of the person's own gift, skill, or resources. Once God is excluded from sole honor or not thanked in the evaluation process, pride is given an open door.

Peer Pressure

Closely linked to pride as a subtle hindrance to worship is peer pressure. Peer pressure also relies on the human spirit, by preferring the opinion of friends or fellow congregants to what the Spirit may rightfully wish to accomplish in one's life. Instead of blocking out those who may be sitting in the pew alongside and focusing exclusively on the Lord, a victim of peer pressure will fall prey to intimidation. This person will resist the leading of the Lord, instead entertaining a thought similar to this:

- "What will they think if I express myself openly?" or
- "What if I cry? . . . They'll think I did something wrong."

Any time we are controlled by thoughts of another person, or crowd of people, and choose not to enter into the flow of worship, we are obstructed from worship. To be confined by the opinions of others, or by our perception of their opinion, can distract from our need to surrender in the Lord's presence in childlike faith. Such submission to fear of others can become a form of idolatry, just as if we *so* became "soloists" in our individualism that we drew the attention of the congregation to ourselves. Maybe we need to reevaluate our self-perceptions and attitudes toward others' opinions as we worship. Do you struggle with peer pressure when a worship service is convened?

Read James 4:7. To whom are we to submit?

Whom are we to resist?

The enemy always strikes our minds through psychological warfare. Resist his fiery darts, relative to peer pressure, and he will flee.

Preoccupation

The final hurdle to worship is preoccupation. This hurdle centers on one's lack of discipline, thinking about the events of the week instead of entering into worship with abandon. The mental discipline of "focusing on Jesus" is a rare jewel we can offer the Lord. It's a part of our "sacrifice of praise" in the twentieth century. Our culture is inundated with sound—with noise, with a flurry of information, which, in effect, tends to lower our ability to concentrate. We must override that trend and require ourselves to think—to remain on task for longer periods of time. What does 1 Peter 1:13 say about this?

At worship, let's choose to concentrate upon the Lord. Discipline is like exercise—the more you practice, the stronger the muscles.

IN SUM

Preparing for worship is a sacred trust. Not unlike a husband who carefully plans an anniversary excursion for his wife, personally and lovingly attending to details, similarly, let us who desire to respond to the call to worship our Lord lovingly look to the details relative to our heart's preparation before we enter into the sanctuary.

Fanny Crosby touched the nerve of the dynamics of willingness to enter into God's presence in humility and awe when she penned,

"I am thine, O Lord,
I have heard Thy voice
And it told Thy love to me;
But I long to rise in the arms of faith
And be closer drawn to Thee.
Draw me nearer, nearer, nearer blessed Lord . . ."

1. *Spirit-Filled Life Bible* (Nashville, TN: Thomas Nelson Publishers, 1991), 1960, "Kingdom Dynamics: Worship and Praise."
2. Ibid., 1790, "Word Wealth: 2:19 foreigners."
3. Ibid., 1890, "Kingdom Dynamics: The Sacrifice of Praise."
4. *Worship His Majesty* by Jack W. Hayford. Copyright © 1987. Word, Inc., Dallas, TX. Used with permission.
5. Graham Kendrick, *Learning to Worship As a Way of Life.* (Minneapolis, MN: Bethany House Publishers, 1984), 189.
6. *Spirit-Filled Life Bible*, 1915, "Word Wealth: 15:7 care."
7. Ibid., 1806, "Word Wealth: 4:8 good report."
8. Bob Sorge, *Exploring Worship* (New Wilmington, PA: Son Rise Publishing and Distributing Co., 1987), 101, 102.

Lesson 6/Singing as Glorious Praise

Psalm 100 opens in a magnificat of timeless importance—

> Make a joyful shout to the LORD, all you lands!
> Serve the LORD with gladness;
> Come before His presence with singing.

From each phrase let's lift one idea that will frame the intent and dialogue of this chapter.

 AT A GLANCE

Psalm 100:1, 2		
Verb	**Phrase**	**Application**
Make	a joyful shout (noise)	1. This is a command. 2. The understood subject—*You* 3. The issue is not aesthetics. The issue is participation—happy involvement.
Serve	the Lord with gladness	1. This is a command. 2. The understood subject—*You* 3. Praise is a method of service. Take pleasure in doing so!

Come	before His presence with singing	1. This is a command. 2. The subject—*You* 3. Singing clearly directs our attention (mind, emotion) toward the Father.

Taken phrase by phrase, these potent, relevant words are foundational in our understanding of the importance of worship—as the event.

The *first* phrase is entirely inclusive. "Make a joyful shout," or noise. The salient feature of this phrase is that everyone is included, not just the relatively smaller portion of any congregation who may have musical talent. The implication is not a performance of stunning perfection but one of gusto—robustness, enthusiasm—even fun! God desires that everyone get "into the act." And that includes you and me.

The *second* phrase, "Serve the LORD with gladness," builds on the importance of enjoyment. Joy is contagious. It spreads like wildfire. It's resultant characteristics are transforming. In an environment where joy released becomes joy multiplied—

The doldrums lift,
The discouraged bounce back,
The downcast regroup,
The burdened become lighthearted, and
The bound are freed!

Praise, as a facet of worship, is pleasurable and powerful. Joy is strength. Stress is vanquished in a room of praise-oriented song. Anxiety has no place in an atmosphere where God's people unify in worshipful melody. That is why singing is so important in the process of praise.

The *final* phrase, "Come before His presence with singing," augments the crucial nature and role of singing as an agent of spiritual release. Singing bursts barriers—real and imagined. Singing levels the playing field. Singing liberates. Singing is something we can all accomplish, regardless of health or socioeconomic status, for singing brings us together through a common lyric and a purposeful, unified focus.

As a medium of expression, music is peerless.

The Scripture is laden with examples in which the song provided motivation to press on in faith or in which singing served as a means of returning thanks when a victory was achieved. Judson Cornwall writes, "Singing renews faith and courage in the midst of adversity. . . . Singing can give us endurance spiritually, emotionally and physically."[1] Singing is a glorious way of praising the Lord. Regardless of which side of the battle you are on—just beginning or gloriously ending— singing praise is viable, even necessary.

LET'S DEFINE PRAISE

If worship is an umbrella, praise is the center pole that we hold. Praise is a meaningful facet in the process and event of worship. Praise is a verbal act. Terry Law elaborates, "Thanksgiving relates more to what God has done, while praise relates to who God is."[2]

Read Psalm 63:3, 4. What motivates praise?

From this verse, how do we know praise is a verbal activity?

Read Psalm 50:23.

Praise _____ God.

What is the implication of "order[ing]" our "conduct"?

Read Psalm 103:1, 2. What way of blessing the Lord, shown in these verses, may become an ongoing conversation piece for us?

List some benefits of the Lord as seed thoughts for future conversations.

-

-

-

-

We may praise God with our voice. We can even use our daily conversations and conduct to effect praise, honoring the Lord for His deeds in our life. Having testified of the Lord's blessing throughout the week, our praise on Sunday, in the worship event, takes on a deepening understanding, as experience reinforces theology.

Read Psalm 47:7.

     FAITH ALIVE

Sing Praises with Understanding. The word "understanding" (Hebrew *sakal,* "prudent or cautious, and hence, intelligent") is linked to wisdom and prosperity. Proverbs 21:16 provides contrast to such understanding: "A man who wanders from the way of understanding will rest in the assembly of the dead." But when we "sing praises with understanding," we are giving testimony to God's love for us and our love for Him. Life results instead of death. Others, listening to us praise God, hear testimony of our salvation and our joyful relationship with Him, which often leads to their own salvation.[3]

Have you experienced times of "singing with understanding," when the worship on Sunday bore witness, either to a need you had at that time or to give you a vocabulary to testify to God's provision in your life? Describe an occasion when a song brought "understanding" alive or focused in words a heartfelt concern.

Is there a relationship between walking with the Lord during the week and praising Him in congregational singing on Sunday? How could you link the two?

Praise is accomplished through our speech and through our song. Read Psalm 149:1–4. Why do you suppose the psalmist entreats us to sing a new song? List two reasons.

a.

b.

Obviously instruments as recorded in verse 3 are important in accompanying our singing. Is it necessary that instrumentalists be skillful? List two reasons.

a.

b.

Unskilled or limited abilities in church music ought never to be scorned. But neither should an "anything goes" attitude be tolerated when it causes more distraction *from* than attention *to* praising God.

WORD WEALTH

Sing praises, *zamar.* To make music, sing praises; to sing songs accompanied by musical instruments. *Zamar* occurs more than forty-five times, mostly in Psalms. There seems to be a special affinity between *zamar* and stringed instruments. The most important derivative of *zamar* is *mizmor* (a psalm, or song accompanied by instruments). Musical instruments are an integral part of praise and worship.[4]

Does singing please the Lord? (v. 4) Why?

Read Psalm 33:1–3. What does the Scripture say about the praise of those who live uprightly? (v. 1) Why do you think this is?

What is the admonishment for those who accompany worship? (v. 3)

Read 2 Chronicles 5:13. The instrumentalists and vocalists, according to this verse, were as _____. That presupposes skill and practice. Then what happened?

 FAITH ALIVE

Praise has many facets, as does the very character of God. There are seasons for expressing joy and seasons for mourning—times in which we celebrate a triumph and times when we praise Him in the valley, by faith, for His ability to work a miracle. There are times when we feel like praising God and times when we invoke the will and, regardless of our emotional state, praise Him simply because He is worthy.

There are times for the "joyful noise"—a congregation of laity lifting simple voices and pure hearts, and times for the "skillful"—rehearsed choirs and orchestras garbed in tuxes and gowns, proclaiming the wondrous birth of Jesus in a city-wide summons to a regal Christmas pageant.

In all of our worship, however, of ultimate importance is the attitude that motivates our every expression of praise—our unity in heart and spirit with other believers and with our God. It is by this that our Lord is truly glorified and honored. For more on this, read Graham Kendrick's *Learning to Worship as a Way of Life.*

BIBLICAL MODELS FOR PRAISE

Throughout the Word, we find numerous examples of God's intervening when His people sang praise. Consider two accounts:

- David
- Paul and Silas

David

David knew the power of music. As a teenager, he perfected his artistry as a harpist while tending sheep. He redeemed his time by worshiping the Lord and playing music. How was he to know how important that activity would be in framing his future? Literally, his worship-as-a-daily-"process" paved the way to an eventual worship-as-a-high-"event" in Israel.

Read 1 Samuel 16:14–23. How does music play a part in this story? Be specific.

List the six characteristics of young David as described in this passage. (v. 18)

a.   d.

b.   e.

c.   f.

Of those characteristics, which one seems to be most important? Why?

What are the implications for us in coupling a music gift with the Lord's anointing?

Regardless of your musical talent, an important truth is resident in this story. Music, anointed of the Lord, can lift the spirit, distract incoming evil thoughts, break evil bonds, and focus attention on the Lord. When you are blue, plug in a praise tape or, if you can, sit at the piano and play a hymn. When you are sick in body or mentally challenged, let music soothe your soul. Do not rest on the arm of the flesh while lying in silence. Transform your residence into an altar by incorporating Christian music into your battle or your recovery process.

Paul and Silas

Often, we sing praise in times of prosperity and in comfortable surroundings. However, God responds to our song when it rises out of uncomfortable adversity as well. Examine the story of Paul and Silas in Acts 16:16–34 as an example.

Why were Paul and Silas imprisoned?

In jail, Paul and Silas rejoiced. How can you explain their resiliency?

What was the effect of their praying and singing hymns at midnight?

What is the correlation for you and me, in terms of singing praise when we are down and "in jail" (figuratively or literally)?

 FAITH ALIVE

Praise Springs Open Prison Doors. Study [Acts 16:25, 26 as an] example of the power of praise, even in difficult circumstances. Beaten and imprisoned, Paul and Silas respond by singing a hymn of praise—a song sung directly from the heart to God. The relationship between their song of praise and their supernatural deliverance through the earthquake cannot be overlooked. Praise directed toward God can shake open prison doors! A man was converted, his house-hold saved, and satanic captivity overthrown in Philippi. Today, as well, praise will cause every chain of bondage to drop away. When you are serving God and things do not go the way you planned, learn from this text. Praise triumphs gloriously![5]

The application of this story is profound. Hymns of faith open prison doors. Are you imprisoned by a bondage of fear? Sing. Sing praise to God. Have your plans temporarily failed? Have you been sidetracked in your attempt to serve the Lord? Sing. Sing praise to God.

Your testimony of endurance, while under stress, may cause an onlooker to ask, "What must I do to be saved?"

So sing. Sing praise to God.

Throughout the Scriptures, biblical characters sang songs in spirited worship and praise. Investigate the significance of one or more of the following:

    AT A GLANCE

FAMOUS SONGS IN THE BIBLE	
Where	**Purpose of Song**
Exodus 15:1–21	Moses' song of victory and praise after God led Israel out of Egypt and saved them by parting the Red Sea; Miriam joined in the singing, too
Numbers 21:17, 18	Israel's song of praise to God for giving them water in the wilderness
Deuteronomy 32:1–43	Moses' song of Israel's history with thanksgiving and praise as the Hebrews were about to enter the Promised Land
Judges 5:2–31	Deborah and Barak's song of praise thanking God for Israel's victory over King Jabin's army at Mount Tabor

2 Samuel 22:1–51	David's song of thanks and praise to God for rescuing him from Saul and his other enemies
Song of Solomon	Solomon's song of love celebrating the union of husband and wife
Isaiah 26:1	Isaiah's prophetic song about how the redeemed will sing in the New Jerusalem
Ezra 3:11	Israel's song of praise at the completion of the Temple's foundation
Luke 1:46–55	Mary's song of praise to God for the conception of Jesus
Luke 1:68–79	Zechariah's [Zacharias's] song of praise for the promise of a son
Acts: 16:25	Paul and Silas sang hymns in prison
Revelation 5:9, 10	The "new song" of the 24 elders acclaiming Christ as worthy to break the seven seals of God's scroll
Revelation 14:3	The song of the 144,000 redeemed from the earth
Revelation 15:3, 4	The song of all the redeemed in praise of the Lamb who redeemed them[6]

As a special study, read each episode and the song it evoked. See how many situations might have an application to you or a situation of which you are aware.

THE BLESSING OF SINGING

As an art form, there must be something valid about singing. After all, it has stood the test of time. Songs, as a means of communing with God, are found throughout the pages of the Scripture. "In 85 places in the Bible we are exhorted to sing praise to the Lord."[7]

A closer examination of the blessing of singing reveals interesting data. From the field of music therapy, I have learned that singing may positively affect an Alzheimer's patient. Note the following:

- "Patients who have lost the ability to talk coherently often retain the ability to sing lyrics to familiar songs (Novick, 1982)."[8]
- "Music has also been found to increase alertness without increasing agitation (Dietsche & Pollman, 1982)."[9]
- ". . . Singing and other musical activities will not only increase an Alzheimer's patient's enjoyment, but may also assist in slowing the progression of the disease (Bower, 1967)."[10]

Singing, like humor, is a natural medication. Those who couple the emotion with the will communicate on a more profound level. When the songs speak of our Lord Jesus Christ, there is added dimension. Songs that are committed to memory through repetition are not affected by disease as quickly as the verbiage of the present. That seems to illuminate a facet of the Scripture spoken by Jesus, "I will never leave you nor forsake you" (Heb. 13:5).

An Alzheimer's patient may not remember current reality, but Jesus is still with that individual through their memorized Scripture and song material. What are the implications for you and me who are still in reasonable health?

Beyond personal health issues, singing is also a blessing for groups of people. A worship event is reinforced by hearty, participative congregational singing. Again, from a music therapist:

- "Exposure to music in group situations enhances self-confidence, self-awareness, emotional relief, pleasure, communication . . . interpersonal behavior."[11]

It may be that a congregation that sings together, forgives together.

- "Involvement in group singing was shown to stimulate, perhaps promote trust and cooperativeness among the participants."[12]

Clearly, singing creates a forum that God delights in. He is able to work on us as we sing—correcting faults, lifting issues that need forgiveness, ministering confidence, pouring oil, recasting dreams, renewing vision. Cornwall wrote, "So often it is during praise time, when we have heated our spirits in worship and have the touch of the presence of God around us, that sublimated thoughts, desires, and attitudes rise to the surface."[13] How wonderfully therapeutic to sense the warm bath of the Spirit, cleansing away the dirt in our lives, as we sing praise and worship material in His presence!

THE BENEFITS OF SINGING PRAISE

Closely associated with the blessings of singing are benefits. Singing ministers to people. New believers are given a marvelous vocabulary for expressing their praise. Seasoned veterans are constantly being encouraged by the addition of new songs, adding variety to their worship.

Singing hymns teaches doctrine. Singing worship choruses teaches Scripture. Singing gospel songs reinforces the testimony of believers.

Read Ephesians 5:15–20. Why should we make the most of every opportunity? (v. 16)

How can we make the most of every opportunity to worship? (v. 20)

What are ways of verbalizing thanks to God? (v. 19)

 FAITH ALIVE

Encouraging One Another in Praise. [Ephesians 5:18, 19] instructs interaction in our praise. Paul tells the Ephesians to "[speak] to one another," using psalms and hymns and spiritual songs. Entering a gathering of believers, even with a small offering of praise, our worship begins to be magnified as we join with others. Their voices encourage us, and we inspire them. Separation from the local assembly deprives a person of this relationship and its strength. Let us assemble often and praise much—encouraging one another in praise.[14]

The apostle Paul refers to the incorporation of three different types of songful worship as a means of fulfilling the directive in verse 18—to be filled continually with the Spirit:

Psalms are scriptural lyrics in song.

Hymns are humanly inspired lyrics in song.

Spiritual songs are impromptu rhythmic lyrics given by the Holy Spirit in one's language or in "tongues" (see 1 Cor. 14:15).[15]

List contemporary examples:
Psalms   Hymns
•   •

•   •

•   •

•   •

IN SUM

Singing of songs and hymns and spiritual songs is a beneficial activity for all believers. It is cathartic. Once an anointed time of singing has occurred, it is easier for a pastor to teach. We are more sensitive to the Word of God after singing.

Singing promotes unity and purifies attitudes. Those who sing may live a little closer to the Cross. For singing encourages believers in their faith. You know, it is impossible to get closer to the Cross without being touched by its life-changing power. Perhaps that is why Paul wrote,

I will sing with the spirit,
And I will also sing with the understanding.
                                    —1 Corinthians 14:15

1. Judson Cornwall, *Elements of Worship* (South Plainfield, NJ: Bridge Publishing, Inc., 1985), 128.

2. Terry Law, *The Power of Praise and Worship* (Tulsa, OK: Victory House, Inc., 1985), 135.

3. *Spirit-Filled Life Bible* (Nashville, TN: Thomas Nelson Publishers, 1991), 795, "Kingdom Dynamics: Sing Praises with Understanding."

4. Ibid., 878, "Word Wealth: 149:3 sing praises."

5. Ibid., 1659, "Kingdom Dynamics: Praise Springs Open Prison Doors."

6. *Life Application Bible* © 1988, 1989, 1990, 1991 by Tyndale House Publishers, Inc., Wheaton, IL 60189. New Testament Life Application Notes and Bible Helps © 1986 owned by assignment to Tyndale House Publishers, Inc. Used by permission. All rights reserved.

Life Application is a registered trademark of Tyndale House Publishers, Inc.

7. *Worship His Majesty*, by Jack W. Hayford. Copyright © 1987, Word, Inc., Dallas, TX, 225. Used with permission.

8. Kristine A. Olderog Millard and Jeffrey M. Smith, "The Influence of Group Singing Therapy on the Behavior of Alzheimer's Disease Patients," Journal of Music Therapy, Vol. XXVI, No. 2, Summer 1989, 59.

9. Ibid., 59, 60.

10. Ibid., 60.

11. Anat Anshel and David A. Kipper, "The Influence of Group Singing on Trust and Cooperation," Journal of Music Therapy, Vol. XXV, No. 3, Fall 1988, 146.

12. Ibid., 146.

13. E. Judson Cornwall, *Let Us Praise* (Plainfield, NJ: Logos International, 1973), 29.

14. *Spirit-Filled Life Bible*, 1794, 1795, "Kingdom Dynamics: Encouraging One Another in Praise."

15. Ibid., 1794, note on 5:19.

Lesson 7/Body Builders!

Americans are crazed about exercise. And is it any wonder? Exercise is clearly linked to weight loss and reduced coronary disease. Exercise keeps us fit. Exercise strengthens the heart. Exercise stimulates a feeling of well-being.

Inherent in those statements are assumptions worth examining. Interestingly, the same thoughts could be articulated about biblically based worship modalities. Worship keeps us fit. Worship strengthens the heart. The more we exercise scriptural models for our worship, the stronger our heart for God. As physical exercise strengthens and invigorates our bodies, so worship renews our mind, in a spiritual sense. Exercise increases an individual's stamina, so work may be accomplished which is energy-consuming and difficult. One who is fit can go distances that would tire or injure an unfit person.

Worship is the exercise of our spirit. The more time we spend in His presence, the more audible His voice; consequently, the more accurately we fulfill His will. Figuratively speaking, the worship "event" is the weight room where spiritual athletes work out, in preparation for the "race" (Heb. 12:1). Serious athletes train carefully in a rigorous routine year round. Twice a month is not enough. The benefit of exercise is to be found only in weekly repetition. In other words—"use it or lose it!" Practice. So it is with the worship "event"—regular, weekly attendance is the only way to grow spiritually. Sporadic attendance will simply frustrate your growth potential. One other note: athletes train the entire body, not just the arms, legs, or stomach muscles. So it is with spiritual exercise; the strong Christian incorporates the entire body into the worship of our heavenly Father.

Let's discover the joy of:

• Lifting Holy Hands
• Standing in Awe
• Kneeling in Deference
• Shouting in Jubilation
• Singing in the Spirit

The body language of Scripture is an important element in the practice of worship.

LIFTING HOLY HANDS

Any form of body language reframes the mind. Moving about heightens our senses. This is basic anatomy. In school, we lift our hand in order to answer a teacher's inquiry. In sports, we lift our hands to receive the ball. In thanking a friend for a gift, we extend our hands in gratitude. Similarly, in the worship event, it is only logical to raise or extend our hands in order to inquire of the Lord or to receive from His bounty, or to express our thanks. And that is scriptural.

Read Psalm 63:3–5. The combination of verbal praise with hands raised seems to bless the Lord. Why?

The process satisfies the participant as well. Reflect on this. Explain.

Read Psalm 134:1, 2. Where are we told to lift our hands? (v. 2)

When one lifts his or her hands, where does one's focus naturally turn? Discuss the significance of that phenomenon.

Read Psalm 141:1, 2. David prayed to the Lord at night. Why is that a good idea?

If nighttime prayer prepares one to sleep peacefully, what is the significance of raising one's hands in the process?

FAITH ALIVE

In verse 2, the lifting of hands is correlated with the evening sacrifice. Though it refers to an ancient priestly practice, it is just as appropriate for us today. An evening sacrifice can be a valuable ritual in the life of a believer. It is simply a prayer where we return all that God has invested in us to accomplish His will that day. Human beings were not created to receive adulation. Retaining praise for or to ourselves will inflate our self-perception. After all, God imparted our gifts. He loaned us our talents. As servants of His kingdom, our role is to daily reflect His grace, as we borrow from His investment in our lives.

Therefore, proper stewardship of any success, compliment, or award received, while on kingdom business or otherwise, involves returning that act of gratitude to the Lord in prayer—at the end of the day. It is natural, then, that along with prayer, the evening sacrifice, one would lift holy hands stating, "Here, Lord, this is really for You."

Read 1 Timothy 2:8 and Psalm 134:2. How is the act of raising holy hands a sign of submission and dependence?

Isn't it hard to doubt that on which we are dependent? Elaborate.

Write a concise statement about the reasons for raising hands in worship or prayer.

STANDING IN AWE

The orchestra has just tuned. The lights have dimmed. A hush falls over the audience. Suddenly, a side stage door swings open and the conductor enters the concert stage. Immediately, the orchestra rises. The body language of that musical ensemble signals worth, respect, and honor.

So, too, in worship—when the Ancient of Days enters, often the people of God will rise in awe.

Read Psalm 122:1, 2. Where did David stand, in terms of his worship? (v. 1) Why?

Read Psalm 134:1; 135:1–3. Analyze your patterns of practice. When do you stand in church?

- •
- •
- •

• • •

Is standing meaningful at those times? Why? (or why not?)

Read Matthew 6:5. Why did Jesus rebuke the hypocrites for standing while they prayed?

FAITH ALIVE

Hypocrites, *hupokrites.* In Bible days actors wore masks, which included mechanisms for amplifying the voice. Since the dramas were questions and answers, the word describing the dialogue was *hupokrinomai,* to reply or to answer. *Hupokrites* is one who is playacting, reading a script, or one who puts on an act. The *hypocrite* conceals his true motives under a cloak of make-believe.[1]

Is there a time when standing may be inappropriate for that, or any other reason?

"Worship should engage every part of our being."[2] There are times when standing is entirely appropriate, and by doing so, the believer's sense of worship is heightened. Standing immediately sends a signal to the brain—"Beware! Someone of notoriety has just arrived."

As significant as standing is in the acknowledgment of worth, so kneeling is in the acknowledgment of respect.

KNEELING IN DEFERENCE

The scenario is classic. Imagine it with me: Boy meets girl. They fall in love. And then, on a warm, fragrant evening in May, the boy kneels down on one knee and adoringly asks, "Will you marry me?" They live happily ever after.

We all know the imagined scenario, and yet, it warms our heart to simply recount it in preparation for this phase of our study. Arguably, kneeling is a gesture of love—a self-effacing act of deference and devotion. In our culture, we kneel out of respect. We kneel when we are in love.

Read Psalm 95:6, 7. What happens when a believer kneels before the Lord? (v. 6)

What is the significance of kneeling?

AT A GLANCE

KNEELING	
Truth Psalms Teaches	**Action** Psalms Invites
Showing Respect for God Humble postures in worship should reflect a humble attitude of heart.	**Humble yourself** before the Lord through bowing and kneeling in worship. **Open your heart** to Him and to His will.[3]

Read Ephesians 3:14. What did Paul do when he bowed his knees?

Why is bowing our knees important when we pray?

What kind of prayers do you pray when you actually bow your knees, taking time to focus in that manner?

Kneeling serves as a testimony of our belief. Elaborate on this valuable form of body language, as expressed in Philippians 2:9–11.

FAITH ALIVE

Faith Exalting Jesus' Lordship. Scholars note that the word "confess" means "to acknowledge openly and joyfully, to celebrate and give praise" (Thayer/Wycliffe). This eloquently and beautifully stated text is a great point of acknowledgment for all who would learn the power of faith's confession. The exalting and honoring of our Lord Jesus Christ is our fountain-head of power in applying faith. The Father honors Him first, then those who confess His Son as well (John 12:26). All humans, angels, and demon spirits will ultimately bow the knee to Jesus, rendering complete and final homage. That confession of every tongue will one day be heard by every ear as He receives ultimate and complete rule. But until that day, our confession of Jesus Christ as Lord invites and receives His presence and power over all evil whenever we face it now. And as we declare His lordship—in faith—His rule enters those settings and circumstances today.[4]

Kneeling naturally slows us down so that we may carefully measure our words to the Lord. Shouting—that is, speaking aloud, declaratively and joyously—is active and assertive. It "gets the adrenalin moving" in celebration of His goodness!

SHOUTING IN JUBILATION

Imagine a scene from a World Series baseball game: It's the bottom of the ninth inning—a key hit causes the fans to shout in response to the player's skill in a clutch situation. Victory is realized. The shout declares the fact!

Should it not be on occasion in the church? Shouting is not done often. However, there are unique occasions when a shout is the perfect release of emotion, expressing the joyous affirmation of God's faithfulness as observed by His children.

Shouting is biblical.

Read Psalm 47:1, 2. Usually shouting is a voluntary response to an action, event, or awareness one perceives. Which is the case here? (v. 1)

What triumphs might we rejoice over? historically, through Christ? presently, by His grace in our lives?

Read Psalm 35:27, 28. List two reasons to shout.

•

•

Why should the Lord be magnified?

 KINGDOM EXTRA

Happy, Holy, Healthy, and at Peace. God is pleased when His servants prosper! The Hebrew word, translated [in Ps. 35:27] as "prosperity," is laden with meaning: "safety, wellness, happiness, healthiness, peacefulness." In fact, this word usually is translated "peace"; when your needs are met, you are at peace. Moreover, if God is pleased with the prosperity of servants, what must He be with the prosperity of His own children—those who are purchased by the blood of Jesus and adopted as His own? Think how thrilled God must be when we—His own children—prosper in every aspect of our lives.[5]

Examine your own life. When has God prospered you? Did you feel like shouting? Why or why not?

Comment on ways a "shout" may take other forms—a cheer, an audible "Hallelujah," a simple verbal statement of thanks. Not all will always shout, but what does Psalm 107:2 say?

Read Psalm 81:1. What reasons does the passage following this verse give for this command? Apply parallels to your life.

God is our strength. He compensates for our frailties and empowers us to succeed. Realizing His efforts on our behalf evoke strong emotions at times, a "joyful shout" may well be in order!

Are you willing to shout?

Is God worthy?

To climax this point, remember: How will Christ return? (1 Thess. 4:16)

SINGING IN THE SPIRIT

The tuneful hymn begins,

> There is a place of quiet rest,
>   near to the heart of God—
> A place where sin cannot molest,
>   near to the heart of God.

Singing in the Spirit is a very sacred, special activity. One has often entered into the throne room, so to speak, when mere human words are no longer sufficient in expressing heartfelt awe and adoration. So the Spirit begins to sing through us—magnifying the Father and the Son in holy verbiage. That is a facet of worship, which, for me, is always edifying.

Paul practiced it in his prayer and praise. Read 1 Corinthians 14:15; Ephesians 5:19. Notice it was appropriate and not abnormal.

Speaking in tongues and singing in the Spirit build the believer and minister to the Lord. They are spiritual gifts for encouragement and strengthening. Whenever I am confused, I pray or sing in tongues. Whenever fear grips my spirit, I pray or sing in tongues. Whenever I am in His presence, in a time of corporate worship—and the worship is flowing, I love to pray or sing in the Spirit.

That gift is available for you. In fact, all the elements of worship through body language suggested in the Scripture are relevant for our walk with Christ. He enjoys our praise. He is exalted when we offer praise and worship in childlike abandonment.

The place of "spiritual songs" is important to consider today, as an awakening of "the song of the Lord" (spontaneous choral worship in song) or "singing with the Spirit" (1 Cor. 14:15) is occurring. Insight is given in Jack Hayford's book *Worship His Majesty*. As a concluding point of study, respond to this brief article.

Singing Spiritual Songs

There are wide differences in definition of "spiritual songs," and I don't want to appear either ignorant or ciritcal of any of them. But I want to discuss my opinion that "spiritual songs" were the apostle Paul's reference to a distinct music form unique to the Church. It was one which would help fulfill the prospect of God wanting to give everyone their own song of praise to Him.

Spiritual songs have been defined as informal choruses, choral anthems, simpler more personal statements of faith or brief, uncomplex odes of worship. But I propose that they were—and are—a new music form unavailable until the New Testament, until Christ's full redemption allowed the Holy Spirit to dwell in mankind. Clearly, early believers sang "spiritual songs" of worship. But what were they?

Hodais pneumatikais, the exact words in both Ephesians 5 and Colossians 3, is usually translated "spiritual songs." The first word is simply "ode," the Greek term for any words which were sung. But the second word—*pneumatikais*—seems to be the key to the full meaning of this phrase.

Pneumatikais—an obvious cognate to *pneuma* (spirit)—is most easily defined and understood noting its use elsewhere in the New Testament. For example, Paul uses this word when introducing the subject of spiritual gifts in 1 Corinthians 12:1 (literally *pneumatika*—"spiritual things"). Later in his appeal to the Galatians concerning their duty to restore fallen brethren, the word also appears: "You who are spiritual ones . . ." (*pneumatikoi*) are assigned the task of that restoring ministry. Although *pneumatika* occurs over twenty times in the New Testament, those two texts give us something of a basic picture. *Pneumatika* seems to indicate Holy Spirit-filled people of character and charisma: Their *character* is noted in the Galatian text: "you who are *spiritual ones* restore the fallen . . ."; their *charisma* (in the sense of their functioning in the charisms—gifts of the Holy Spirit) is indicated in their apparent acceptance and response to "spiritual things," that is, manifestations of the Holy Spirit's gifts.

These factors alone would not finalize a definition, except for the fact that in this same context Paul discusses "singing with the spirit and with the understanding." It is here in this classic passage, 1 Corinthians 12—14, as the apostle corrects their abuse of glossolalia, that he also discusses singing of a distinctly Holy Spirit-enabled nature:

> For if I pray in a tongue, my spirit prays, but my understanding is unfruitful. What is the result then? I will pray with the spirit, and I will also pray with the understanding. I will sing with the spirit, and I will also sing with the understanding.

His distinguishing singing "with the spirit" from "singing with the understanding" points to what "spiritual songs" may have meant in the first-century church: an exercise separate from yet complementary to the singing of psalms and hymns.

Since the general passage beginning in 1 Corinthians 12:1 and the specific text beginning in 1 Corinthians 14:1 *both* use *pneumatika* to describe the kind of subject matter being dealt with, it follows that the distinct type of singing referred to as being "with the spirit (pneuma)" could be the same as "spiritual songs." I would not be so bigoted as to oppose another interpretation, but I propose that the whole of the New Testament context supports the definition of "spiritual songs" as being Holy Spirit-enabled utterances—

—which were sung rather than spoken;

—which were most commonly to be a part of one's devotional life;

—which were explained or interpreted if exercised in corporate gatherings; and

—which were so desirable as to have Paul assert his personal "will" to practice them—"I *will* sing with the spirit also."

I would not preclude the possibility or desirability of spiritual songs being in the native language of the worshiper nor suggest that one (glossolalia or native tongue) was preferable to another. But it does seem clear that the Holy Spirit is at work in this worship expression, doing something distinctly valid and valuable.

The practicality of this exercise is readily understandable when we remind ourselves how God has given the gift of worship for our edification as well as for His exaltation. It shouldn't surprise us if the gift of song for worship, praise, thanksgiving and adoration should provide one of its three forms in an arena of free, completely original, personal expression. Such spontaneity in personal worship may allow me the liberty of lyricizing my own heart's joy or pain, lifting it on a melody I spontaneously breathe forth. To so sing removes the restrictions of poetic rhyme and meter or musical rhythm and form. A practical, scriptural and desirable thing occurs: a previously unsung song—*a new song*—is wafted forth from worshiping lips, adoring Him and releasing the soul to broadened dimensions of glorifying the Creator.

Thus the spiritual song rounds out a triad of music forms given to the Church:

- In *psalms*, we declare His *Word* in song; we learn and rehearse the eternal, unchanging Word of His revealed truth in the Scriptures.
- In *hymns*, we announce His *works* in song; we praise Him and review His attributes, testifying to His goodness as experienced over the centuries.
- In *spiritual songs*, we welcome His *will* in song; giving place to the Holy Spirit's refilling, and making place for His Word to "dwell richly" within.[6]

Let's review.

 AT A GLANCE

BODY LANGUAGE IN WORSHIP		
Language Type	**Vital Scripture**	**Demonstrates**
Lifting Hands	I will lift up my hands in Your name. (Ps. 63:4)	Submission, Dependence, Open to receive

Standing	You who stand in the house of the LORD. . . . (Ps. 135:2)	Respect, Honor, Worth
Kneeling	Let us kneel before the LORD our Maker. (Ps. 95:6)	Humility, Devotion, Adoration
Shouting	Shout to God with the voice of triumph! (Ps. 47:1)	Affirmation, Enthusiasm, Joy
Singing in the Spirit	I will sing with the spirit, and I will also sing with the understanding. (1 Cor. 14:15)	Submission, Sensitivity, Love

IN SUM

Body language heightens our expressions of worth to the Savior. As you ponder this lesson, may you be encouraged to apply these truths of Scripture to your pursuit of Christlikeness, for as Paul Hoon wrote,

"It is easier to act one's way into a new feeling than to feel one's way into a new way of acting. . . . Actions such as kneeling, bowing of the head, repeating words or songs familiar from the past can induct attitudes not initially present. Feelings are seldom under the control of the will, but actions are. . . ."[7]

1. *Spirit-Filled Life Bible* (Nashville, TN: Thomas Nelson Publishers, 1991), 1414, "Word Wealth: 6:2 hypocrites."

2. Terry Howard Wardle, *Exalt Him* (Camp Hill, PA: Christian Publications, 1988), 41.

3. *Spirit-Filled Life Bible*, 847, "Truth-in-Action through Psalms (Book Four: Psalms 90—106)."

4. Ibid., 1804, "Kingdom Dynamics: Faith Exalting Jesus' Lordship."

5. Ibid., 783, "Kingdom Dynamics: Happy, Holy, Healthy, and at Peace."

6. *Worship His Majesty*, by Jack W. Hayford. Copyright © 1987. Word, Inc., Dallas, TX, 150–152. Used with permission.

7. Paul Waitman Hoon, *The Integrity of Worship* (Nashville, TN: Abingdon, 1971), 318, 319.

Lesson 8/Be Still and Know

Anyone who has walked with God for a period of time realizes that there is no prepackaged routine for His manner of communication. God is not predictable. He is sovereign. He moves when and where He chooses. He is Lord: we are His servants.

Accordingly, we must be with Him on a regular basis in order to perceive His directions—His will. The process of waiting in His presence for purposes of exaltation and communication is important to discuss in our development as a vibrant worshiper.

A worshiper bestows homage to the one being honored. There are times of active praise—singing, lifting our hands, shouting, kneeling—and times of silent devotion. The contrasts are striking, while the motives and objectives are synonymous.

Often, in times of active praise, worshipers will invoke the presence of the Lord. The joyous singing in one accord is appealing to God. The word confirms this: "You [God] *are* holy, enthroned in the praises of Israel" (Ps. 22:3). As the flow of choruses comes to an end, someone may pray, or a message by the Spirit may be given (see 1 Cor. 14:26).

It is at this moment that we juxtapose active praise with silent devotion.

Although quiet, the mind should be steadfastly fixed on the "word" now being spoken. A mature worshiper knows when to participate actively and when to participate devotionally. Even when one is silent, listening to a prayer or processing a spontaneous "word" from the Holy Spirit, the kind of worship we commend focuses on the moment and willfully avoids distractions.

In the worship event, there is a place for active participation and silent devotion. Similarly, in the worship process, walking with the Lord daily as we develop Christlikeness, there is also a time to sing and a time to be silent.

In previous lessons we have discussed, at length, the role of active praise with emphasis on body language participation. Now it is time to concentrate on the less tangible, yet equally important role of listening for the voice of God as we pursue His calling in our lives.

Praise has as a purpose the bringing of us all to a closer place in God's presence. Once in His presence, we may be wise to develop a proficiency at being silent, in order to hear His Word, and subsequently to obey. This would apply both to when we are in church ("event") and when we are at our quiet time, throughout the week (a part of the "process").

Define "being still" (Ps. 46:10) as it relates to being in God's presence.

Being still is the act of _____

_____ while in God's presence.

While "still," list ways God can teach us or confirm His presence and His will. (Clue: Analyze Psalm 46.)

-

-

-

-

FAITH ALIVE

As a grown son, I can still say, being with my earthly father is always comforting. All of my life, his strength and integrity have created within me a sense of security. I know that if I go to him with a question, problem, or prayer request, he will offer proper guidance and faithful prayer.

So it is for us all with our heavenly Father. Being in His presence, sensing His deity and infinite wisdom, is also comforting. Regardless of the storm around us, He has an ability to calm the stress and remind us of His unfailing love. Being still amidst His strength is a productive exercise, ". . . for My [that is, His] strength is made perfect in weakness" (2 Cor. 12:9).

CREATE THE OPPORTUNITY

Before God can speak, we have to be listening. Listening is a matter of self-discipline. A proportional return on our investment is available to us, as believers, should we choose to learn how to listen effectively. Simply stated, the more we listen the greater the chance of hearing God's voice.

This may be accomplished through the biblical practice of meditation. Properly incorporating meditation into our worship process affords believers daily encounters with our Father in heaven. Consequently, we are strengthened, guided, and empowered for service.

Meditation has three aspects: salutation, introspection, and consecration.

Let's examine each in light of the Word of God.

Salutation

A salutation is a greeting. We typically answer the telephone with the salutation, "Hello." We may write a letter, beginning with the salutation, "Dear Friend." In our quiet time of meditation, consider beginning with a warm greeting.

Read Revelation 3:20. The word picture presented here is classic. Christ is knocking at the door of our heart each morning. Will you let Him in? How will you greet Him? List examples. Be creative and free—He's your Savior and Friend.

Apply this word picture from Revelation 3:20 to your daily quiet time. How can a salutation, which is a form of worship and praise, naturally evolve into a deeper, more intimate meditation?

NOTE: Remember, "Christian Meditation" is biblical—totally unlike pagan practices which seek to (a) focus on an inner place humanistically, (b) contact a "spirit-guide" demonically, or (c) escape consciousness transcendentally or hypnotically. True meditation is focused on Christ, His Word, God's love; and is fully conscious, alert, and alive in the Holy Spirit.

(J.W.H.)

Introspection

Following a greeting, which may include an informal yet respectful, loving description of Christ's worth to you, the next step in Christian meditation is introspection. The act of introspection involves self-examination, confession, and forgiveness of sin and a realignment to godly standards of conduct. This realignment occurs through a personalization of Scripture.

In the introspection phase of meditation, a passage of Scripture is chosen and pondered deeply. Richard Foster notes, "The simplest and most basic way to meditate upon the text of scripture is through the imagination . . . We are desiring to see, to hear, to touch the biblical narrative. In this simple way, we begin to enter the story and make it our own."[1] This process is time-consuming. In fact, the German theologian, Dietrich Bonhoeffer recommended spending a whole week on a single text![2]

Introspection is challenging. Introspection requires time in order to ponder. Introspection often produces penetrating questions.

Read Psalm 19:14. What do you think it means to have our words and meditation acceptable in His sight? (Note the sources: *mouth* and *heart.*)

In this phase of meditation, realizing our imperfections is inevitable, how should we process our shortcomings and sins? (Rom. 8:1)

What is the result of seeking forgiveness? (1 John 1:7, 9)

KINGDOM EXTRA

"Acceptable" Speech Before God. This oft-quoted verse [Ps. 19:14] attests to the importance and desirability of our words and thoughts being consistent with God's Word and will. The text literally says, "Let what I <u>speak</u> and what my heart murmurs to itself be a delight to You, Lord." Clearly, the acceptability of our words in God's sight is dependent upon their being consistent with what our hearts feel or think. The truth of this text urges us to always speak the kind of words that confirm what we believe or think in our hearts about God, His love, and His power. If we believe, yet contradict that belief with careless words from our mouth, it is not acceptable in God's sight. Remember the lesson of Cain's sacrifice (Gen. 4:1–7): what is unacceptable is not only faithless and fruitless; it may also become deadly.[3]

Apart from asking forgiveness for sins, including careless speech, during the introspection phase of our meditation, we may naturally proceed through a listing of questions about our present life situation, its direction, and our need for wisdom, discernment, and guidance.

Read James 1:5. To whom does God give wisdom? What is His response to them?

What kinds of situations do you face needing God's wisdom?

How do we need to ask to receive God's wisdom? (James 1:6–8) Outline the significance of each of these three verses.

WORD WEALTH

Reproach, *oneidizo.* Originally, to behave in a very juvenile and immature way, describing youngsters who make fun of, tease, and taunt each other. Then the word came to denote mocking, ridiculing, scolding, insulting, and using

words angrily or sarcastically. James 1:5 assures us that God
gives without reminding us of our unworthiness.[4]

During our introspection, we open ourselves to God's
forgiveness and ask for God's wisdom. A logical step should
follow—consecration.

Consecration

Once God imparts wisdom to us, it is time for us to commit to His instruction—to yield to the path of His prompting.
Consecration is an act of setting apart for ministry. It is a type
of dedication and affirmation. We agree to obey His directives
for the day . . . for a lifetime.

Let's review.

After greeting the Lord, personalizing the Scripture, sensing our frailty, seeking forgiveness, asking for wisdom, hearing
His response—it is now time to act. The consecration is our
promise to fulfill what we have been instructed.

Read John 8:47a; James 1:22. Is the hearing of God's
Word enough? Why?

What do you think it means to be a doer of God's Word?

When have you heard a word from God and done something tangible about it? How did you feel? How can you make
that example habitual?

Creating an opportunity for God to speak is critical in our
process of understanding the importance of being still in His
presence. And yet, there is more.

LISTEN TO GOD

Eugenia Price wrote, "The voice of God is always speaking
to us, and always trying to get our attention. But His voice is a
'still, small voice,' and we must at least slow down in order to

listen."[5] Slowing down our activity and blocking out the many sources of sound pollution that distract and confuse is challenging work, to be sure. Yet to overcome the distractions is to begin to focus on the Lord. Then we must work at listening.

Listening is hard work.

To become a good listener requires concentration. We must resolve to stop talking and stop controlling.

We must become more comfortable with a pause—a golden moment of silence. We must shed the sound-byte mentality of the media and wait on the Lord.

You see, God is not in a hurry. We are. We rush everywhere. However, as Oswald Chambers once wrote, "Rush is wrong everytime; there is plenty of time to worship God."[6] Therefore, in order to hear from God, we must relax and accommodate His divine clock. Patience is a productive virtue in the process.

Read Isaiah 40:31. List the four promises to those who wait on the Lord.

•

•

•

•

Read 1 Samuel 10:1–8. How long did Samuel have to wait for the Lord?

Did God ever tell you to wait?

Was it easy?

After His answer, could you more easily understand His purpose in making you wait? Discuss honestly.

Read Psalm 27:14. What is the benefit of waiting on the Lord?

How does waiting strengthen our heart? (Read Psalm 62:5–8 for insight.)

As we wait upon God (Ps. 37:7a), we increase our chances of hearing His voice. We also may expect His provision of strength, because we are acknowledging our dependence on Him. He is our refuge. He is our defense. He is our salvation. Those are faith statements. God responds to faith. He is a rewarder of those who diligently seek Him (Heb. 11:6). Faith produces rest.

HEAR HIS STILL SMALL VOICE

An unforgettable scriptural example of God's voice speaking to a person occurs in the story of God's revelation to Elijah. Here we are introduced to a poignant expression, "a still small voice," focusing quietness and intimacy with God, preliminary to power and victory.

Read 1 Kings 19:11–18. List the three actions of nature in which the Lord was not present. (vv. 11, 12)

-
-
-

List comparative contemporary distractions we may have to get by in order to hear the "still small voice" of God.

-
-
-

FAITH ALIVE

Because God is sovereign, He has the capacity to surprise us in His method of communication. He may speak to you through a renowned speaker at a large conference, or He may whisper to you via an anonymous servant in your everyday routine.

Whether He speaks through the wind, an earthquake, or fire, or whether He waits for us to calm down so He may simply whisper, we can hear from Him if only we take the time and remain sensitive.

Read Hebrews 2:1–3. What happens if we do not take heed to the things we have heard from God? (v. 1)

Simply hearing a word from God is not enough. God's directives to us always demand a decision. What is that decision?

What is the penalty for disobedience?

In brief, hearing the "still small voice" presupposes an ability to listen carefully as well as a willful determination to obey the instruction, once given (Deut. 30:20).

WHAT WILL HE SAY?

Each time God speaks to us, His word is fresh. The specifics may vary, dependent upon our need, yet I can assure you of two principles regarding the nature of God's directives that are rock-solid:

1. He will never speak to you in terms that contradict His eternal Word, the Bible.

2. He will always lead you with a sense of peace.

Let's focus on each principle.

First, the Bible is "conduct specific." The Ten Commandments carefully delineate a pattern of behavior that is value driven (Ex. 20:1–17). Jesus also spoke of the greatest commandment, "Love your neighbor as yourself" (Lev. 19:18). Further, all the New Testament writings speak of relational issues in great detail. Consequently, bank on the fact that God will not speak to you leading you to circumvent or ignore His Word. That is to say, "God will never tell us to engage in any activity or relationship that is inconsistent with the Holy Scripture."[7] That is why Bible study is so important in the worship event and in the worship process.

Second, a yardstick measuring the veracity of a "word" you perceive as coming from the Lord is found in the condition of your spirit as you meditate on that word. As a result of thinking about a word from God, are you nervous . . . perplexed . . . fearful? Or, are you content . . . restful . . . peaceful? Author Charles Stanley aptly writes, "When God speaks, one of the most prevalent signs is a sense of calmness in the spirit."[8]

Read Philippians 4:7. How can peace surpass your understanding?

Why is that process beneficial when under stress or in shock? Personalize.

As you pray, asking God for wisdom in making a decision or direction about your future, believe that He will answer your prayer. Confirm His answer, as it is accompanied by a prevailing sense of peace, for "peace has always been the umpire for doing the will of God."[9]

IN SUM

This lesson has developed the theme of silent devotion. In tandem with active praise, the believer is edified and God is honored. Aspects of a healthy devotional life include meditation, a proactive method of listening to God speak, and a realization of the two principles God will not violate when, in fact, He does speak.

To conclude, let us remember the immortal words of Scripture regarding the encounter Elijah had with the Almighty:

Then He said, "Go out, and stand on the mountain before the LORD." And behold, the LORD passed by, and a great and strong wind tore into the mountains and broke the rocks in pieces before the LORD, but the LORD was not in the wind; and after the wind an earthquake, but the LORD was not in the earthquake; and after the earthquake a fire, but the LORD was not in the fire; and after the fire a still small voice. So it was . . . Elijah heard it . . .

—1 Kings 19:11–13a

1. Richard J. Foster, *Prayer: Finding the Heart's True Home* (New York, NY: Harper-Collins Publishers, 1992), 147.

2. Ibid., 146.

3. *Spirit-Filled Life Bible* (Nashville, TN: Thomas Nelson Publishers, 1991), 768, "Kingdom Dynamics: Acceptable Speech Before God."

4. Ibid., 1895, "Word Wealth: 1:5 reproach."

5. Nancy Corbett Cole, *Tapestry of Life: Devotions for the Unique Woman* (Tulsa, OK: Honor Books, 1992), 84.

6. This quotation is taken from *My Utmost for His Highest* by Oswald Chambers. Copyright © 1935 by Dodd Mead & Co., renewed © 1963 by the Oswald Chambers Publications Assn., Ltd., and is used by permission of Discovery House Publishers, Box 3566, Grand Rapids, MI 49501. All rights reserved.

7. Charles Stanley, *How to Listen to God* (Nashville, TN: Thomas Nelson Publishers, 1985), 51.

8. Ibid., 61.

9. Edwin Louis Cole, *The Potential Principle* (Springdale, PA: Whitaker House, 1984), 31.

Lesson 9/Worship as Contemplation

There is an inexorable link between meditation and contemplation in the life of a serious student of worship. Biblical meditation is centered in the process of worship—as defined by a daily, quiet time. Contemplation, the focus of this lesson, is a more specific form of meditation. For contemplation is to our prayer life what intimacy is to a marriage. After a while, a married couple begins to "know" each other in the "non-verbals"—a subtle, more fulfilling form of communication.

Before discussing contemplation further, it may help to briefly recapitulate lesson 8. We saw meditation as the art of spending time alone with God, with three parts in the meditation sequence: salutation, introspection, and consecration. The focus of biblical meditation we see in this passage from the Word is a call to "pondering" in a personal way.

Read Psalm 1:2, 3. When does the psalmist meditate? What does that indicate?

Contemplation relates to the actions determined as a result of a person's thoughtfulness and quiet reasonings. How would you release or define this in your own life as you see the link between meditation and contemplation?

WORD WEALTH

Meditates, *hagah.* To reflect; to moan, to mutter; to ponder; to make a quiet sound such as sighing; to meditate or contemplate something as one repeats the words. *Hagah* represents something quite unlike the English "meditation," which may be a mental exercise only. In Hebrew thought, to meditate upon the Scriptures is to quietly repeat them in a soft, droning sound, while utterly abandoning outside distractions. From this tradition comes a specialized type of Jewish prayer called "davening," that is, reciting texts, praying intense prayers, or getting lost in communion with God while bowing or rocking back and forth. Evidently this dynamic form of meditation-prayer goes back to David's time.[1]

This is an important beginning place, because "contemplation" builds on biblical meditation, as deeper thought and perspective flows from time given to consideration and review.

What does Psalm 1:3 intimate about the stability of one who practices Christian meditation?

What is the promise for one who meditates? Define biblical prosperity. (See Eccl. 11:6 for assistance.)

As we grow in grace, we naturally desire more and more of God's presence. We progress from talking to listening—from meditation to contemplation. "Contemplative prayer is the one discipline that can free us from our addiction to words. Progress in intimacy with God means progress toward silence."[2]

Read Psalm 62:1. Are you comfortable being silent in the presence of an acquaintance or newfound friend? Why?

Contrast the sense of need to "entertain" casual acquaintances with the comforting freedom to simply be quiet around best friends. Then relate this phenomenon of intimacy to our relationship with the heavenly Father.

The key to any relationship's flourishing is spending quality time together. The more we abide, the deeper the bond.

Read John 15:4, 5. In a spiritual sense, what does it take to produce fruit in our lives? List examples of abiding in Christ, in contemporary terms (as compared with the agricultural terms in Jesus' analogy of the vine).

Reflect on the final phrase, "for without Me, you can do nothing." What does that mean? How is it relevant to our spiritual growth and development?

Read Psalm 24:3, 4 and Matthew 5:8. Can one develop a pure heart in any way other than through abiding in Christ? Explain carefully.

A pure heart is one in which sin has been dealt with and motives have been examined. Under the microscope of the Holy Spirit, during a contemplative quiet time, these faults are focused—so we can seek forgiveness and cleansing. How do you arrange to spend quality quiet time with God? Is there room for growth in your relationship? Look inside yourself, and specify the ways.

Read Proverbs 8:34, 35. Fill in:
Blessed is the man who _____ to me, _____ _____ at my gates, _____at the posts of my doors. For whoever _____ me _____ life, and _____ _____ from the LORD.

Relate the verbs you just filled in to our discussion of contemplation. What insight is gleaned from these verbs? (List them in order.)

     FAITH ALIVE

>   The author Eugene Peterson writes, "I know it takes time to develop a life of prayer: set-aside, disciplined, deliberate time. It isn't accomplished on the run, nor by offering prayers from a pulpit or at a hospital bedside. I know I can't be busy and pray at the same time. I can be active and pray; I can work and pray; but I cannot be busy and pray. I cannot be inwardly rushed, distracted, or dispersed. In order to pray I have to be paying more attention to God than to what people are saying to me; to God than to my clamoring ego. Usually, for that to happen there must be a deliberate withdrawal from the noise of the day, a disciplined detachment from the insatiable self."[3]

The reward for withdrawing from the noise of the day is rest—the rest of the Lord.

THE LORD'S REST

Those who meditate on God's Word, contemplating its application, are able to transcend anxiety and worry and, ultimately, rest in the Lord.

Read Matthew 11:28–30. How is rest imparted to the life of a believer? (vv. 28, 29)

Studying and applying principles seen in Jesus' life is therapeutic. He managed stress, misunderstandings, conflicts, ridicule, and even death with great dignity. Briefly list areas in which you could become more like Christ by "learning of

Him" and consequently improve in your interpersonal relationships and conflict management skills.

-

-

-

-

What is a yoke? How is Christ's yoke easier than the one of traditional religion?

Evangelist Ron McIntosh writes, "Real rest always brings me back to the understanding that I do not have to make anything happen. I only have to be obedient to Christ."[4] As we learn about Christ in our devotional life, it becomes easier to obey Him. Knowledge releases obedience, for knowledge places God's power in juxtaposition with our circumstances. Knowing that He will take care of us is an incentive to obey.

Read 1 Kings 8:56–58, 61. Has God's word ever failed? How does that make you feel?

Does God's word have a track record? How do you know? (v. 57) Is that phenomenon true in your family heritage or in a friend's godly family line? Explain.

What must we do to invoke His blessing? (vv. 58, 61) List verbatim.

-

-

-

Rewrite those three conditional phrases in your own words. Then apply to your current walk with Christ. When are you successful? Why? Where can you use improvement? Be specific.

Write	Application
•	•
•	•
•	•

One might deduce a formula for bringing closure to the concept of contemplation: *obedience = rest*. Even Jesus needed rest. And Jesus found rest in His solitude, where He often heard from God and determined to obey.

Read Mark 1:35. Why did Jesus need to pray?

Why did Jesus need to pray in a solitary place?

What does His model prayer life say to you? Contemplate.

Read Isaiah 30:15. When are believers strong?

How are these qualities enhanced, thereby forming character in our lives?

Read 1 Thessalonians 5:16–18.

AT A GLANCE

Truth 1 Thessalonians Teaches	Action 1 Thessalonians Invites
Guidelines for Growing in Godliness Godly believers live unto God and for God. They seek to honor and reflect God in everything they think, say, or do. Godliness lives quietly, is absorbed in doing good for others and works productively. Godliness has a good reputation with unbelievers. Godliness is knowing the commands of Scripture and doing them.	**Understand** that successful Christian living consists of 1) work that flows from faith, 2) labor that flows from love, and 3) patient endurance that is born of living hope. **Insure** that your life is thus characterized. **Be faithful to intercede** for other believers and other congregations. **Live your life** in order to please God, not yourself. **Live** a quiet, peaceful life. **Never gossip. Be diligent** in whatever work you have chosen to do. **Earn** a good reputation with unbelievers. **Conduct your life,** being alert and self-controlled. **Practice** the commands of Scripture.[5]

Resting in God enhances our daily speech. Those who learn to trust Him, believing He will come through, do not need to murmur, complain, or assassinate someone's character. Their hope is not in their boss or their neighbor. Their confidence is in the Lord.

Worry is banished in times of meditation. Fear is expelled in the closet of prayer. Those who contemplate on the Word find themselves praying without ceasing (1 Thess. 5:17). Chuck Swindoll notes that "those who rest in the Lord take on a mind-set that refuses to struggle or allow worry to eat away at them."[6]

How does Hebrews 4:9–11 explain the ways of real rest?

WHAT KEEPS US FROM REST?

Simply stated, when we remove Christ from His place at the center of our lives, relying on our own finite decision-making capacity and hardening our heart to His will, we find ourselves restless. Without God at the helm, there is no peace, no lasting satisfaction. Consequently, there is no rest.

In his book, *Keep the Flame Burning*, Ron McIntosh details five key words—each signifying a behavior or mind-set—that may provide rest or steal it, depending on how each is used. Here is a chart noting these concepts for your consideration:

 AT A GLANCE

FIVE S'S OF THE REST MESSAGE

KEY WORD	CONNOTATION	
	Pro	Con
1. Schedule	Every schedule must contain a balance of recreation and rest.	Christians are susceptible to schedule abuse.
2. Stress	We must minister out of His strength and not our faculties. (Our responsibility is to wait on Him. . . to obey, trust and believe.)	Most men and women of God let burdens turn into a need "to make things happen." (taking on in their own flesh the responsibility to do what God desires)

3. Sleep	A person was made with the need to restore and recreate the energy of this human body.	One of the devil's oldest tricks is to get you to do too much, if he cannot get you to do too little.
4. Sin	We must repent of any sin —especially any that attempt to carry out His plan by our own effort.	Perhaps the greatest sin of spiritual leaders in history was the desire to do a right thing in a wrong way.
5. Spirit	There are no great men, only humble men whom God has chosen to use greatly.	Yet, somehow, it seems we forget.[7]

With this chart as a prompter, what applications would you make to move toward a greater "rest" in your (1) relationship with the Lord, (2) with present circumstances, or (3) with past pain?

In Sum

Who can adequately place a price tag on the value of resting in the Lord? In a world of chaos and confusion, God's people are often healthy and hearty. Health is a by-product of diet. A spiritual diet of meditation and contemplation fosters hearty energy for living a victorious Christian life.

We may be tested and tried. We may endure hardship or be grossly misunderstood. Yet, if we can manage to keep our eyes on the Cross, we will survive—even triumph.

One of the reference points of London is the Charing Cross. It is near the geographic center of the city and serves as a navigational tool for those confused by the streets.

A little girl was lost in the great city. A policeman found her. Between sobs and tears, she explained she didn't know her way home. He asked her phone number, she didn't know that either. But when he asked her what she knew, suddenly her face lit up.

"I know the Cross," she said, "show me the Cross and I can find my way home from there."

So can you.[8]

—Max Lucado

1. *Spirit-Filled Life Bible* (Nashville, TN: Thomas Nelson Publishers, 1991), 753, "Word Wealth: 1:2 meditates."

2. Richard J. Foster, *Prayer: Finding the Heart's True Home* (New York, NY: Harper-Collins Publishers, 1992), 155.

3. Eugene H. Peterson, *The Contemplative Pastor* (CTi, Carol Stream, IL, 1989), 29.

4. Ron McIntosh, *Keep the Flame Burning* (Tulsa, OK: Vincom, Inc., 1992), 181.

5. *Spirit-Filled Life Bible*, 1831, "Truth-in-Action through 1 Thessalonians."

6. Charles Swindoll, *Growing Strong in the Seasons of Life* (Portland, OR: Multnomah Press, 1983), 210.

7. Ron McIntosh, *Keep the Flame Burning* (Tulsa, OK: Vincom, Inc., 1992), 190–195.

8. Max Lucado, *And the Angels Were Silent* (Portland, OR: Questar Publishers Multnomah Books, 1992), 43.

Lesson 10/Worship as a Healing Balm

The term "balm" may be a curious word to you. Years ago, I remember singing the song, "There is a balm in Gilead," from the scripture found in Jeremiah 8:22. Gilead was an Old Testament locale where oils and spices for medicine were developed.

In a very real sense, music is a type of balm, for it has healed and soothed the human spirit for centuries.

Music therapists know that. Worship leaders and pastors also know that music facilitates the healing process. Music, as a form of worship, can create an environment in which we focus on God's power rather than our present circumstances. That is an act of faith. It pleases God. In fact, our worship invokes His presence among us, and "In [His] presence *is* fullness of joy" (Ps. 16:11).

What do you think those words from Psalm 16:11 mean?

In God's presence, we are made whole—restored, renewed, released. God is all-powerful. Jesus is the Great Physician. Music, touched by the Holy Spirit, is a roadway on which we walk into the very presence of deity and experience His power and healing.

So many of us especially sense God's presence in church. A church is a *sanctuary* in the sense that all are welcome, all are accepted, all are safe. In today's hostile, secular environment, it is meaningful to attend church.

A church is also a *hospital*—a M.A.S.H. unit, if you please. Incoming vehicles escort wounded and broken people, and the pastor and lay leaders go to work. Sometimes a listening ear suffices. Other times further pastoral care is needed. Yet active participation in the worship event while in extended counseling, dynamically reinforces the healing process. Worship is beneficial because of its transforming characteristics.

Paul Anderson wrote, "Sometimes struggling people will find help only when they begin to look outside themselves toward heaven. Worship, because it focuses outward, can bring a healthy corrective to narcissism."[1]

Our culture is narcissistic, or selfish. Whenever people focus inwardly rather than outwardly (from themselves), and upward (to God), they practice idolatry. Their self-centeredness is a form of idolatry, and the god-less-ness of it all is self-destructive.

Selfishness is a prime factor in the exponential divorce rate prevalent in our society. The wounds inflicted upon a family when spouses separate and divorce are monumental. But when broken and discouraged, the "balm of Gilead" is available to bring forgiveness, healing, and restoration. Worship is a component of that process. Worship is the canvas on which the Lord can paint a new future for you!

Read 2 Corinthians 5:17. What are examples of your old things that are passed away in Christ?

Consider your present. What "old things" need to be passed away?

Come to Jesus now, and let Him make "all things . . . become new" in your present need for healing balm, as certainly as He has done this in your past.

 WORD WEALTH

New, *kainos.* New, unused, fresh, novel. The word means new in regard to form or quality, rather than new in reference to time, a thought conveyed by *neos.*[2]

According to Isaiah 61:1–3, when the anointing comes from God, what nine spiritual manifestations may occur?

a.

b.

c.

d.

e.

f.

g.

h.

i.

 WORD WEALTH

Anointed, *mashach.* To anoint, to rub with oil, especially in order to consecrate someone or something. Appearing almost seventy times, *mashach* refers to the custom of rubbing or smearing with sacred oil to consecrate holy persons or holy things. Priests (Lev. 8:12; 16:32) and kings (2 Sam. 2:4; 5:3; 1 Kin. 1:39) in particular were installed in their offices by anointing. In Exodus 40:9–14, the tabernacle was to be anointed, as well as the altar, the laver, and the high priest's sons. The most important derivative of *mashach* is *mashlyach* (Messiah), "anointed one." As Jesus was and is the promised Anointed One, His title came to be "Jesus the Messiah." Messiah was translated into Greek as *Christos,* thus His designation, "Jesus Christ."³

The promised power in Isaiah's prophecy applies to our worship times. Now, draw your own conclusions regarding the importance of attending church services, noting the metaphor of the church being a hospital and this Isaiah passage's delineation of God's power to heal. Apply each phrase as you can see an analogy to present circumstances.

In an atmosphere of worship, God's healing power may take different directions. Let's investigate three:
- Promoting Forgiveness
- Bringing Physical Healing
- Assisting Psychological Recovery

PROMOTING FORGIVENESS

"God therapeutically touches a soul that is intensely focused on worship."[4] Worship fosters intimate communication. Worship is really dialogue with God. We sing. He speaks. We open up and He pours in. The reciprocity inherent in worship promotes our willingness to please God by turning from sin and forgiving all those who have offended or hurt us.

For example, an individual who has been wounded by an unkind remark or a rude action and is unwilling to forgive the perpetrator carries an emotional bruise with him or her into a worship service. As the worship choruses flow, the bruised individual may soften as the Lord pours in grace upon grace. Consequently, the individual becomes willing to forgive. That supernatural transformation is a work of the Spirit as we sing praise to God.

Worship promotes forgiveness. Read Isaiah 42:2, 3. Jesus' ministry was prophesied in this prophetic figure. Through the dialogue of worship, Jesus may speak to a worshiper about his or her need to forgive.

List ways in which we may be bruised by unacceptable behaviors of those with whom we associate.

In worship, when an area of unforgiveness is brought to our conscious mind by Jesus, what are our options? (See Matt. 5:23, 24.)

Which option pleases God? Why?

Examine your own heart. As you worship, have you recently ignored the gentle touch of the Holy Spirit to seek forgiveness? Act upon that nudge. Pray. Effect restitution. Anticipate greater freedom next Sunday!

Read Hebrews 4:16. How ready is God's forgiveness! Define the key words here.

Read John 20:23. What does it mean to forgive sins? (Examine Matt. 18:27 for help.)

What is the penalty of retaining sins? (Consider Matt. 18:28–35 as insight.)

FAITH ALIVE

Often in a worship experience, a thought may pass through our minds reminding us we haven't forgiven someone. Has this occurred to you? If we activate that thought by seeking forgiveness from the Lord, peace ensues. The sense of peace is like an aspirin soothing away a headache. It feels so good not to hurt any longer.

Yet to ignore the prodding of the Holy Spirit is to make the sin that originally hurt us, a part of us. That is double jeopardy! We were offended by a rude or selfish act. We now harbor unforgiveness *and* that rude, selfish act as well. As we continue to resist the forgiveness process, the act that offended us grows into a root of bitterness—eventually infecting all our life and relationships.

This is noted in the secular world as well. For example, a child abuser often testifies to being abused as a child. An adult child of an alcoholic often displays similar dysfunctional characteristics of the alcoholic parent in his or her business and family relationships—even though the adult child may not consume alcohol.

Consequently, we cannot afford the "luxury" of unforgiveness. It is too expensive. It is too risky. It is, potentially, too devastating.

The beauty of a worship event is that we are often confronted with unforgiveness, resident in our hearts, in a gentle manner. If we can adopt a policy of listening to and not ignoring the Holy Spirit, the worship experience will be liberating and the "balm" of forgiveness will be healing. "Sometimes we may not be able to praise God ourselves, but if we can be around others who can . . . God can still begin His healing work."[5]

Physical Healing

Spirit-filled believers affirm the contemporary reality of the doctrine of divine healing. Healing is scriptural. Healing is relevant. In the worship event, healing is an inheritance.

Read Matthew 9:18–26. Retell this story in your own words. Notice the role of worship in relationship to healing.

Now, how do you feel about the story? about Jesus? Could this account be repeated in our time? Why?

Read Matthew 8:1–4. How did the leper's worship prepare him for healing?

Word Wealth

Willing, *thelo.* To wish, desire, will, take delight in. It carries the idea of being ready, preferring, and having in mind. A related New Testament word is *boulomai,* a stronger expression of the will, signifying the determinant will deliberately exercised.[6]

What was Jesus' response? (v. 3) Why is His response no different today? (Hint: Heb. 13:8)

Is there anyone in need of healing in your circle of influence? Would worship assist their faith as they are drawn into Christ's presence? Consider Hebrews 10:19–23.

Read Luke 17:11–19. What did the ten lepers request? (v. 13)

What was the response of the lepers to their healing?

How can you see ingratitude as debilitating to our relationship with Christ?

KINGDOM EXTRA

Healing as They Went. The nature of some healing as "progressive" is noted in the words "as they went, they were cleansed." [See Luke 17:12–19.] The ten lepers' healing affords several lessons: 1) Not all healing is at the moment of prayer. Instant healings are often expected, whereas this illustrates the healing "in process" over a period of time following prayer. 2) Jesus' directive "Go . . . to the priests" not only indicates His affirmation of the Law (Lev. 13:1–59). Since the priests were the physicians of that culture, it indicates His approval of persons who have received healings seeing their physicians for confirmation of the healings. 3) The lepers' obedience to Jesus' command is important to note. As they went in obedience, they were healed. When healing is not instantaneous, one ought not to doubt, but find a possible path of obedience. 4) Of that group of lepers healed by Jesus, only one returned to express gratitude. When healing comes, express thanks with praise and worship, and do not be as the nine who failed to return with thanksgiving.[7]

Worship is a potent environment, then, in which healing can occur—healing of the body and healing of the mind.

PSYCHOLOGICAL RECOVERY

The quintessential example of worship music's effect on the mind is captured in David's interaction with Saul, depicted in 1 Samuel 16:14–23.

What was the source of Saul's emotional and mental sufferings?

Were David's musical abilities natural or supernatural? (See vv. 17, 18)

What psychological and spiritual effects did David's anointed worship music have on Saul? (v. 23)

Read 1 Samuel 1—2:11 and analyze the life of Hannah, the mother of Samuel the prophet.

What was Hannah's dilemma? (1:2)

Describe how this situation was made more painful by Elkanah and Peninnah. (1:4–6)

What was the extent of Hannah's depression? (1:7)

Carefully read verses 8–18. Describe the progression of activities.

AT A GLANCE

Truth 1 Samuel Teaches	Action 1 Samuel Invites
How to Tame the Tongue Taming the tongue involves knowing that things you should not say to men may often be said to God.	**Voice** any complaints **only** to the Lord. **Remember** that vindication comes only from the Lord.[8]

How do you know that Hannah loved the Lord? Be specific.

What is the tremendous blessing for loving the Lord as Hannah did? (1:19)

Read Hannah's worshipful prayer aloud. Commit relevant portions to memory.

What lessons can be learned from Hannah's victory over "bitterness of soul"? Be specific.

Has there been a time when worship has had a similar effect on your emotional/psychological state? Testify.

Clearly, worship played an important role in Saul's victory over depression and Hannah's struggle with bitterness. Whether you encounter unforgiveness, have need of a physical healing, or simply feel inadequate, depressed, or embittered— worship is therapy. Worship is cathartic.

Worship hails renewal.

AT A GLANCE

Fill in the column, "Lesson to Learn."

WORSHIP AS A HEALING BALM

Type of Healing	Vital Scripture	Lesson to Learn
Forgiveness	If you forgive the sins of any, they are forgiven them; if you retain the *sins* of any, they are retained. (John 20:23)	_____ _____ _____ _____ _____
Physical	Were there not ten cleansed? But where *are* the nine? (Luke 17:17)	_____ _____ _____
Psychological	She *was* in bitterness of soul, and prayed to the LORD. . . . (1 Sam. 1:10)	_____ _____ _____ _____

MISSION STATEMENT

Write a brief personal mission statement in which you declare your belief in and support of regular worship services. Develop a personal concept of the importance of worship in the life of a believer and list its benefits. The challenge is to keep this statement concrete: simple, direct, personal. The form may be poetry or prose. Limit: 50 words.

IN SUM

Let's close in prayer:

Lord Jesus, Thou knowest me altogether. Thou knowest that I have steadily refused to forgive this one who has wronged me, yet have had the audacity often to seek Thy forgiveness for my own wrongdoing.

The acids of bitterness and a vengeful spirit have threatened to eat away my peace. Yet I have stubbornly rationalized every unlovely motive. I have said, "I am clearly in the right. It is only human to dislike a few people. This one deserves no forgiveness." How well I know that neither have I ever deserved the forgiveness which Thou hast always freely granted me.

So, Lord Jesus, I ask Thee now for the grace to forgive this hurt. . . .

And, Lord, I give to Thee this emotion of resentment which clings as if glued to my heart. Wrest it from me. Cleanse every petty thought.

For these great mercies I thank Thee, in Thy name, who gave me the supreme example in forgiving even those who slew Thee.

Amen.[9]

1. Paul Anderson, "Worship as Pastoral Care," *Leadership*, Summer, Vol. XII, No. 3, 1991, 130.

2. *Spirit-Filled Life Bible* (Nashville, TN: Thomas Nelson Publishers, 1991), 1758, "Word Wealth: 5:17 new."

3. Ibid., 1043, "Word Wealth: 61:1 anointed."

4. Welton B. Gaddy, *The Gift of Worship* (Nashville, TN: Broadman Press, 1992), 47. Used by permission.

5. Michael Coleman and Ed Lindquist, *Come and Worship* (Grand Rapids, MI: Chosen Books, a division of Baker Book House Co., 1989), 70.

6. *Spirit-Filled Life Bible*, 1417, "Word Wealth: 8:2 willing."

7. Ibid., 1550, "Kingdom Dynamics: Healing as They Went."

8. Ibid., 439, "Truth-in-Action through 1 Samuel."

9. Catherine Marshall, *The Prayers of Peter Marshall* (Grand Rapids, MI: Chosen Books, a division of Baker Book House Co., 1982), 45.

Lesson 11/Worship When Answers Aren't Enough

Her name is Sue. She is my friend. In fact, the lessons I have learned from Sue regarding the tenacity of faith, under pressure, are astounding. Let me relate some.

Sue's life was challenging. A failed marriage, teenage children—one dying at 18 of sudden cardiac arrest, another challenged by a learning disability—only begin to tell of the stress factors in her life. Arguably, being a single parent is a tough lifestyle in our culture. Through all these trials, however, Sue managed to stay resilient. And then one day in church she met Art.

Art was a wonderful man. He was the kind of guy described in Scripture as having "no deceit" (John 1:47). I knew Art and his family well. An entrepreneur. Four fine sons. His joy—golf and choir. Art was a jolly man with a smile for everyone. Unfortunately, his wife had succumbed to cancer a couple of years previously. That incident shook Art, but he stayed active in church and bounced back. Time and the family of God are helpful resources in maneuvering through a maze of grief.

And now, it was springtime again.

With the blessing of their pastor, Art and Sue began seeing each other. I'll never forget Art bouncing into the church foyer one Sunday morning with a long-stem red rose in hand. "I can't wait to see Sue, Pastor. We're going to have a wonderful day together!" I watched as he glided through the crowded vestry, oblivious to the clamor, so anxious to find the object of his new-found affection. I mused, "It's a new day for Art!" and smiled.

Their dating continued. A ring followed. And an announcement. Sue was effervescent. They sat together on the third row as though, finally, after much mutual sorrow their lives were going to change. Happiness is a transforming emotional state.

And then, without provocation, the church phone rang. The report: Art had stopped for breakfast one Sunday morning and suffered a fatal heart attack. Gone—six weeks before their wedding. The shock was intense. The ensuing days seemed like a movie in slow motion: the viewing; the funeral. Afterwards, Sue was on the third row—alone.

It was at this point that my pastor-servant role to Sue solidified. As her congregation's minister of music, we had occasional contact, and on one Sunday night, I felt inspired to simply pray for her. In the course of our conversation at the altar, she told me how long the nights were. I suggested a radio—soft Christian music.

"Let it play all night long. As you awaken, it will soothe you. While you sleep, it will cradle you."

With my wife's partnership, I agreed to pray with Sue that Sunday evening for as long as she needed. Slowly, she began to talk a little more and cry a little less. Grief is a process. Sudden grief is even a slower process. Yet Sue found solace in the worshipful music. Her worst time was the night. Music pierced that darkness and communicated Christ's love.

Sue found a song in the night (Ps. 77:6).

Life is risky. Tribulations come. And, as Martin Lloyd-Jones once wrote, "Instead of mere resignation or plucking up one's courage, the Scripture shows that it is possible even under such conditions to be in a state of actual rejoicing."[1]

Sue's trial and movement through it is a solid though somber reminder of how often we all face similar times in our own lives.

Begin, please, with Habakkuk 3:17, 18. List the six maladies Habakkuk recites; proof that life's reversals seem always present even for the most faithful. (v. 17)

-                 •

-                 •

-                 •

Regardless of circumstances, the prophet was optimistic. What shines forth as his secret? How can you explain his perspective?

Read Psalm 30:5b (notice the chapter notes for this verse). React to the metaphor of night turning to morning as "weeping" to "joy" in the life of a believer. Is it truly possible? Does weeping simply "lodge" for a night? How long might such a "night" of the soul be? What have you found?

Define joy in your own words. How does one develop the healthy attitude of joy when sorrows plague like a flood?

Joy is

Now, measure your analysis with the following definition. Are there other meanings of "joy"? What is your feeling about Jack Hayford's definition, based on Hebrews 12:2: "Joy is the settled confidence of the soul which realizes, and can therefore rejoice during hard trials, that beyond the present struggle is God's ordained triumph, and that even the trial is ordained *because* He sees the certainty of His purpose being fulfilled beyond it—unto your ever higher joy!"

    WORD WEALTH

Joy, *gil.* To joy, rejoice, be glad, be joyful. *Gil* contains the suggestion of "dancing for joy," or "leaping for joy," since the verb originally meant "to spin around with intense motion." This lays to rest the notion that the biblical concept of joy is only "a quiet, inner sense of well-being." God dances for joy over Jerusalem and because of His people (Is. 65:19; Zeph. 3:17). The righteous Messiah shall rejoice in God's salvation with an intensity that the psalmist cannot find words to describe (Ps. 21:1). In turn, His redeemed citizens are joyful in their King; they praise Him with dances, with instruments, and with singing (Ps. 149:2, 3). Although everything is wrong in Habakkuk's external world, he is leaping for joy over his fellowship with Yahweh.[2]

Read Nehemiah 8:10. How is joy a strength?

Have you met someone like Sue who has survived multiple tragedies through faith in Christ? Briefly journal their testimony. How have their experiences touched you in a positive fashion?

Charles Trombley says, "It's impossible to have joy in the midst of life's circumstances in your own power. It must be the Lord."[3] With that thought, now read Isaiah 61:1–3 and respond to the following:

Notice the phrase "the garment of praise for the spirit of heaviness." What does this scripture infer about worship?

When should we worship the most? Why?

What does worship do for the downcast?

FAITH ALIVE

"Happiness is based on freedom from stress, absence of problems, avoiding unfavorable circumstances and conflicts, while JOY is the confidence we have that 'greater is He who is in me than he who is in the world.' Therefore, joy doesn't look on outward problems, but inward possibilities.

"It's obedience to this principle that lifts your heavy, mourning soul because you've been anointed with the 'oil of gladness, the mantle of praise, instead of the spirit of heaviness' (Is. 61:1–3). There will be inner JOY because obedient praise always lifts the broken spirit heavenward."[4]

Sadly, too many miss God's best because, when sorrow strikes, they run from worship rather than embracing worship. Worship strengthens us. JOY is found in the presence of the Lord, even when our circumstances are painful.

THE SONG IN THE NIGHT

One way to foster joy in painful circumstances is to allow the Holy Spirit to teach us to sing His "song in the night." This principle of faith found resonance in Sue's heart, during the pain of her bereavement. It is a relevant concept in the life of a vibrant worshiper. For, in our "long nights of the soul," our problems loom larger than life. In darkness and loneliness, stress can magnify and pain intensify. Steadfastness, by its very definition, is a quality of character that is tenacious, choosing to grip God's hand. The steadfast worshiper is, therefore, not dissuaded by temperament, feeling, or situation. By choosing to sing in the face of great stress, one's inner life transforms the outer circumstances. Sensing Christ's resurrection power places our reality into perspective. Note Isaiah's words to the barren woman in Isaiah 54:1–3. *Life* is promised when *song* is present amid lifelessness or shredded hopes. The "song in the night" is not a new phenomenon. It was practiced in the Old Testament. Read Isaiah 30:29a, Psalm 42:8, and 77:4–6 and discover—it's been available for thousands of years and still is today!

Why is a song in the night so comforting?

Can the Spirit inspire the mind to remember a song when we are going through a stressful season of life? Have you experienced such an occasion? Or do you need a song now? Tell the Lord—now; or thank Him for past songs in the night.

List songs which have brought comfort to you in the night. Fill in the chart, noting the name of the song, the nature of your stress, and the manner of your nurture.

The Song	The Stress	The Significance
1.		
2.		
3.		
4.		

Why is it important to remember God's faithfulness in the past?

A song, inspired by the Holy Spirit, can carry a believer through both stress and storm. Often as a student I can remember driving to class playing a favorite, enriching gospel song as I journeyed to the campus to give a recital or take an exam. I may have been up late in study and fatigued, or perhaps nervous about an upcoming presentation; and then as the music played, the hand of God would seemingly touch my shoulder and I would sense peace. The fatigue would flee; the fear vanquished. The reality of "the peace of God, which surpasses all understanding . . ." (Phil. 4:7) would, once again, reframe my mind. I was prepared for the challenge of the day.

The shadow of His wings brings comfort. Read Psalm 63:6–8 and 32:7. Record the psalmist's "style" in dealing with nighttime worries (63:6–8).

What do you think the "songs" described in 32:7 achieve?

IN SUM

Pain is a part of the human experience. As seasons shift, so do our temporal circumstances. The victorious Christian life is not free from pain, but simply free from its debilitating, paralyzing effects. Our Lord Jesus Christ empowers us to live above the pain such that our spirit is renewed, our vision and hope replenished through worshiping Him with the songs He will supply in the "nights" we face.

> *When I remember You on my bed,*
> *I meditate on You in the night watches.*
> *Because You have been my help,*
> *Therefore in the shadow of Your*
> *   wings I will rejoice.*
> *My soul follows close behind You;*
> *Your right hand upholds me.*
> —Psalm 63:6–8

1. D. Martin Lloyd-Jones, "How to Rejoice in Tribulations," *Table Talk*, Vol. 15, No. 12, December, 1991, 34.

2. *Spirit-Filled Life Bible* (Nashville, TN: Thomas Nelson Publishers, 1991), 1344, "Word Wealth: 3:18 joy."

3. Charles Trombley, *Praise: Faith in Action* (Indianola, IA: Fountain Press, 1976), 63.

4. Ibid.

Lesson 12/Lifelong Worshipers

The goal of any adult educational experience is to create an appetite for lifelong learning. A class is finite. So, too, is a degree program. There is a beginning and end point. However, to achieve mastery of any subject requires a lifetime of application and internalization. A true student is able to complete a degree and then continue to learn, perhaps informally, or on the job, by reading, analyzing, and creatively contributing to the field. There is always more to experience.

As a student graduates into the category of a lifelong learner, so as believers we may graduate into the category of becoming lifelong worshipers. Let's target that!

Anyone who commits to a lifelong pursuit of God, via worship, is a disciple in the classical sense of the word; a lifelong worshiper who will continue in the Word, with the intent of doing what it says.

This order of worshiping disciple will connect sincerity to continuity, to being steadfast self-starters. They'll not be persuaded by emotion, gimmick, or charm, but always ruled by that love of Christ "that will not let me go."[1] They can worship when it's raining, when the piano is out of tune, or when they are blue.

You see, lifelong worshipers are determined, zealous to follow Christ regardless of circumstances. They have grown to prioritize Christ in their life until, as Editor Kent R. Wilson has observed, "Worship isn't just a service I attend. It is a life itself lived out before God."[2]

Worship enhances life.

Clearly, worship is a godly habit, which not only glorifies God worthily, but which also nurtures a more preferable future. No matter the crisis, a worshiper has relief. No matter the storm, a worshiper has a raft. No matter the disappointment, a worshiper has a redeemer.

In fact, worship as a life-style—both weekly in the event and daily in the process— allows the believer to "isometrically" fellowship with the Lord. We flex: we relax. That natural ebb and flow allows us to speak to God as well as listen and obey.

In short, worship allows us to trade stress for joy, worry for contentment, and the pain of defeat for the promise of ultimate victory.

Let's investigate.

TRADE STRESS FOR JOY

We all crave a more preferable future. Designing a future that is bright presupposes enhanced coping skills for life's inevitable storms. We need to gain mastery over stress. Worship is a proven vehicle for that phenomenon because a worshiper releases control.

Once God is in control, we may simply relax and enjoy the ride. For, as we abandon our plans for His will, the Word promises joy. Joy in the Christian life is found in obedience to God's principles for conduct. Apply the Word of God to your life and you will rejoice, realize satisfaction and effectively resist temptation.

Read John 15:10, 11. What are the commandments about which John is speaking?

How is Jesus' life on earth a model for us, in terms of being a lifelong worshiper? in terms of trading stress for joy?

How can Jesus' joy remain in us?

Characterize a person whose "joy is full."

A joyful person is an individual of focus and resolve. He/she has determined to focus on modeling Christ to the culture and resolved to resist sin, thereby pursuing a holy lifestyle. "Only those who walk in holiness experience true joy."[3]

Read Psalm 16:11. What is the "path of life"?

What are the assumptions inherent in the idea that "in [God's] presence is fullness of joy"?

Outline Psalm 16, noting the observations about the writer's feelings toward God's ways and works—feelings that feed the psalmist and/or worshiper's confidence by the time he comes to verse 11.

v. 2:

v. 5:

v. 6:

v. 7:

v. 8:

Steadfastness in lifelong learning of the way of worship is often tested by stress. Stress is tension brought about by physical or emotional strain. It can paralyze creativity, test patience, and retard compatibility. The biblical antidote for stress is joy.

Read 1 Peter 1:3–9, noting verse 6 as pivotal. List the three terms used to describe our heavenly inheritance. (v. 4)

•

•

•

What does it mean to be "kept by the power of God"? (v. 5)

  WORD WEALTH

Kept, *phroureo.* A military term picturing a sentry standing guard as protection against the enemy. We are in spiritual combat, but God's power and peace (Phil. 4:7) are our sentinels and protectors.[4]

How is verse 6 an accurate description of our plight as Spirit-filled believers?

List ways in which faith is often tested "by fire"? How have you found testing stressful?

If a test or trial is lived through successfully, what does this passage say about faith's genuineness? (v. 7)

Living through stressful trials and not succumbing to temptation nor full-fledged sin, creates within the believer a joy, which St. Peter describes as "_____ and full of _____" (v. 8). As we overcome, we become stronger for the next trial. Read John 16:33.

Are we promised a life void of tribulations? Why should we be cheerful?

WORD WEALTH

Tribulation, *thlipsis.* Pressure, oppression, stress, anguish, tribulation, adversity, affliction, crushing, squashing, squeezing, distress. Imagine placing your hand on a stack of loose items and manually compressing them. That is *thlipsis,* putting a lot of pressure on that which is free and unfettered. *Thlipsis* is like spiritual bench-pressing. The word is used of crushing grapes or olives in a press.[5]

How did Jesus overcome the world?

How can we overcome tribulation?

Is there any reason to be joyful as you study this passage? Express your thoughts.

FAITH ALIVE

"The very thing you think is a painful proof of God's absence from your life is, in fact, His loving provision to draw

you toward Himself—so that your joy may be full."⁶ It's all a
matter of perspective. We must praise the Lord when we perceive our cup is half full or when we perceive our cup is half
empty. Regardless of our attitude—optimistically or pes-
simistically speaking—He is worthy.

Worship is such a useful aid in recasting our perspective
from the natural to the supernatural, from our limited strength
to His limitless power. For, "Once we've beheld God in worship, we look back down on our world from His perspective.
We find what we thought was a mountain was only a mole-
hill. . . . On the other hand, what we thought was weak, we
learn is actually strong; what we thought foolish is wise."⁷

Our perspective will inform our attitude. Once refreshed,
our proclivity toward defeat by stress is transformed by joy.
Worship creates optimism. Optimistic people are not pre-
tenders, but seers—that is, "ones who see God's promised
hope as a secured victory—in time." (JWH)

TRADE WORRY FOR CONTENTMENT

Worry is an emotional state plaguing our society. If our
confidence is based in economics, politics, or corporations,
worry seems inevitable. However, for the worshiper, confidence is found in the Lord, knowing that His hand is not
short and His power is never constrained. Thereby, the by-
product of the worshiper's focus is contentment amid otherwise wearying circumstance. Read Psalm 139:8–10.

What does David say about the omnipresence of God?

What does that statement evoke within your spirit?

Read Matthew 6:25–34. What are the two formidable
items about which Jesus said not to worry? (v . 25)

Which two analogies from nature did Jesus use to compare our value as human beings? (vv. 26, 28)

Copy verbatim the spiritual antidote for worry. (v. 33)

  WORD WEALTH

Worry, *merimnao.* From *merizo,* "to divide into parts." The word suggests a distraction, a preoccupation with things causing anxiety, stress, and pressure. Jesus speaks against worry and anxiety because of the watchful care of a heavenly Father who is ever mindful of our daily needs.[8]

Read Philippians 4:6–8. Paraphrase verses 6 and 7 in your own words. Then translate the meanings of those verses into crisp statements of your own.

Paraphrase	Synthesis
v. 6	1.
	2.
	3.
v. 7	1.
	2.

Worry is a fruitless exercise. Most of our worries do not even come to pass. Therefore, when confronted with a perplexing thought, reframe your brain to meditate on verse 8. List the phrases. Memorize.

"Whatever things are _____ ,

Whatever things *are* _____ ,

Whatever things *are* _____ ,

Whatever things *are* _____ ,

Whatever things *are* _____ ,

Whatever things *are* _____ _____ _____ ,

. . . meditate on these things."

WORD WEALTH

Good report, *euphemos.* Compare "euphemism" and "euphemistic." A combination of *eu,* "well," and *pheme,* "a saying." *Euphemos* is speech that is gracious, auspicious, praiseworthy, and fair-sounding. It includes the avoidance of words of ill omen. An Old Testament counterpart is found in Proverbs 16:24: "Pleasant words *are like* a honeycomb, sweetness to the soul and health to the bones."[9]

A practical way to trade worry for contentment is to follow the simple, honest advice of Hudson T. Armerding, former president of Wheaton College. Think through this chart which has been synthesized for your study and application.

AT A GLANCE

HOW TO WIN OVER WORRY	
STATEMENT	AMPLIFICATION
1. God knows our circumstances.	1. Reread Psalm 139:8–10.

2. We can't change our circumstances by worry.	2. On occasion in an airplane during a storm, I've worried about whether the plane would make it through. My worrying didn't do one bit of good to help the pilot or stop the storm.
3. The fact is rarely as bad as the anticipation.	3. We fuss about matters, and they don't turn out to be as difficult as we had anticipated while overcome with worry.
4. Not everything has to be pleasant.	4. We serve a providential God who permits things to happen to us for our good. We know this from the book of Job . . .
5. Worriers don't accomplish much.	5. Concentrate on the people of faith in the Bible who were faced with compelling circumstances: a. Abraham—told to go b. Esther—in the face of execution saw the king c. Joseph—in prison d. Deborah—argued with Barak. If these people had been controlled by worry, would they have been effective leaders?[10]

I love the words of Jesus, "With God all things are possible" (Matthew 19:26), so . . . why worry?

TRADE THE PAIN OF DEFEAT FOR THE PROMISE OF ULTIMATE VICTORY

"As finite human beings, we have built-in obsolesence—we are falling apart. . . . Pain is part of the mortality package."[11] Pain comes in many forms: physical, physiological, relational. The effect of worship on our pain is noteworthy. Worship soothes. Worship reprioritizes. Worship transforms our perspective while we suffer from pain—promising an ultimate victory.

What are some promises in the Word of God relative to human pain and ultimate victory.

   AT A GLANCE

Fill in.

SCRIPTURE	PROMISE
Ps. 40:1–4	
Ps. 126:1–6	
Is. 35:10	
1 Cor. 15:53–57	
1 Pet. 5:8–10	
1 John 5:4	

The New Testament story of Jairus in Luke 8:40–56 is an example of a father's pain that was ministered to by Jesus. Read it and answer:

Who was Jairus and why did he fall at Jesus' feet? (vv. 41, 42)

In spite of Jairus's pain, he left his daughter to follow Jesus. Why? Did it take faith to follow Jesus while he was painfully concerned for his daughter? Explain in detail.

Does it take faith to follow Jesus today? What if we are in pain as well? Take time to look at your own experience.

Is following Jesus a type of worship? Discuss.

What is the significance of Jesus' statement in verse 50?

Was Jairus's act of faith worthwhile? (v. 56) How so?

What implications and/or applications can you derive from the account of Jairus?

Jairus experienced a miracle. He followed Christ at a time when his personal life was racked with painful anxiety. It may have seemed risky to leave his dying daughter to worship the Lord, but his faith was noticed by Jesus. Let's ask ourselves, "Is mine?"

Bringing Perspective

Throughout the pages of biblical history, men and women have worshiped the Lord. Some have, indeed, been notable. Others simply anonymous. Following is a chart delineating those whose worship bears emulation.

AT A GLANCE

FAMOUS WORSHIPERS IN THE BIBLE

Old Testament

Where	Purpose of Worship
Gen. 22:1–19	Abraham offered up the ultimate sacrifice of his only son Isaac on Mount Moriah.
Ex. 15:1–21	After the Israelites safely crossed the Red Sea, Moses and the people sang a song of praise to the Lord.
1 Sam. 1; 2	Hannah gave her son Samuel back to God as an act of worship and thanksgiving for answered prayer.
2 Sam. 6:1–23	When David returned the ark of the Covenant to the tabernacle, he danced before the Lord.
1 Kin. 18:20–40	When Elijah prayed, the power of God consumed the altar with fire and all the people fell on their faces and worshiped God.
2 Chr. 20:1–30	King Jehoshaphat appointed singers to go out before the army and sing praises. God delivered the enemy into their hands.
2 Chr. 29	King Hezekiah reestablished the service of worship by ordering the priests to cleanse the temple and offer burnt offerings. The priests sang and played instruments while all the people worshiped.
2 Chr. 34:1–33	King Josiah destroyed the altars of Baal and the wooden images in Israel and thus restored true worship to the people.

New Testament

Where	Purpose of Worship
Matt. 2:1–12	After a long journey, the wise men came to Bethlehem and worshiped the Christ child, honoring Him with expensive gifts.
Matt. 26:30	Jesus and the disciples sang a hymn after the Last Supper before going to the Garden of Gethsemane.
Luke 1:46–55	Mary praised God with a song upon hearing Elizabeth's blessing of her unborn son, Jesus.
Luke 2:36–38	Anna, a widow of many years, prayed and fasted day and night in the temple.
Luke 21:1–4	The widow gave all she had to the temple offering as an act of worship.
John 9:13–41	After the blind man was healed, he worshiped Jesus.
John 12:1–8	Mary, at Simon's house, anointed the feet of Jesus for burial with a costly perfume as an offering of worship.
Acts 16:16–40	Paul and Silas prayed and sang praises to God in prison and the prison doors were opened.

Reviewing the sixteen cases above, select four that address your view of the kind of steadfastness you would hope to cultivate as a worshiper. Express your thinking as a prayer to the Lord.

IN SUM

In every situation, God is worthy to receive adulation and praise. The biblical characters of faith clearly demonstrate that fact. The objective of our entire study together will be realized, if you, the reader, will internalize the truth that,

O Lord, You are *the portion of
my inheritance and my cup;
You maintain my lot.
The lines have fallen to me in
pleasant* places;
Yes, I have a good inheritance.

*I will bless the Lord who has
given me counsel;
My heart also instructs me in the
night seasons.
I have set the* LORD *always before
me;
Because* He is *at my right hand I
shall not be moved.*

*Therefore my heart is glad, and
my glory rejoices;
My flesh also will rest in hope.*
—Psalm 16:5–9

1. George Matheson and Albert Lister Peace, *Sing His Praises* (Springfield, MO: Gospel Publishing House, 1991), 163.

2. Kent R. Wilson, "Monday Morning Worship," *Discipleship Journal,* Issue 70, July/August 1992, (Vol. 12, No. 4), 29.

3. Jerry Bridges, *The Pursuit of Holiness* (Colorado Springs, CO: NavPress, 1978), 154.

4. *Spirit-Filled Life Bible* (Nashville, TN: Thomas Nelson Purlishers, 1991), 1907, "Word Wealth: 1:5 kept."

5. Ibid., 1607, "Word Wealth: 16:33 tribulation."

6. Merlin R. Carothers, *Power to Praise* (Plainfield, NJ: Logos International, 1972), 115.

7. Paul Thigpen, "Who Needs Worship?" *Discipleship Journal,* Issue 70, July/August, 1992, (Vol. 12, No. 4), 34.

8. *Spirit-Filled Life Bible,* 1415, 1416, "Word Wealth: 6:25 worry."

9. Ibid., 1806, "Word Wealth: 4:8 good report."

10. From: *Practical Christianity,* pp. 249, 250. Compiled and edited by LaVonne Neff, Ron Beers, Bruce Barton, Linda Taylor, Dave Veerman, and Jim Galvin. © 1987 by Youth for Christ/USA. Used by permission of Tyndale House Publishers, Inc. All rights reserved.

11. Ibid., 328, 329.